HENRY BRUNTON'S

HIGH

PERFORMANCE

GOLF

*The Serious Golfer's Guide
to Effective Training*

Cover and text design by Beth Farrell

Cover and text layout by Brooke Sumner

Sea Script Company

Seattle, Washington

ISBN: 978-0-9856420-1-3

Library of Congress Card Catalogue No.: 2012940616

First Printing July 2012

Printed in Canada

SEA SCRIPT COMPANY
www.seascriptcompany.com
info@seascriptcompany.com
tel 206.748.0345

Contents

Foreword
by Dr. Rick Jensen

Over the past 20 years, I've had the good fortune to have worked with champions on the PGA and LPGA Tours, and if I've learned one thing, it's that "playing great golf is about much more than perfecting your swing!" Champions throughout the decades have demonstrated that they can "golf their ball" with all kinds of swing shapes. Hogan, Snead, Palmer, Nicklaus, Sorenstam, Woods—could their swings be more different? What's not different is the underlying factors that drove these serious golfers to the top of the game! In *High Performance Golf*, Henry Brunton shines a bright light on what it truly takes to master the game of golf.

For those of you striving to fulfill your golf potential, finding a coach with the knowledge, experience and ability to help you get there is a good first step. You'd think that locating such a coach would be an easy task. Unfortunately, it's not! The reality is that most golf instructors are trained to provide fault-and-fixes golf lessons and not much more. The typical golf instructor will videotape your swing, compare you to their preferred swing model, pinpoint a swing flaw, prescribe a drill or two, and send you on your way. When the fix doesn't work, less serious players question their abilities and often quit the game. More serious players won't quit, but they do begin the endless search for an instructor, a magazine, a book, a training aid or a golf tip that will finally provide them with the eventual remedy to their golfing ills.

Fortunately, you now have that prescription in your hand, and it couldn't have been written by a more qualified person in the game—Henry Brunton! I've had the opportunity to work alongside some of the game's top-ranked golf instructors, from Harmon to Leadbetter to McLean, but when it comes top-ranked golf "coaches," Henry Brunton stands among the best in the world. Intentionally, I differentiate between a "golf instructor" and a "golf coach," and as Henry teaches you more about this distinction in *High Performance Golf*, you will come to understand why many serious golfers never maximize their golf potential.

Henry has traveled the world coaching the game's top players, educating the best coaches, and designing the long-term athlete development programs that will forever change the way golf is taught and learned. Henry's formal education in the sport sciences combined with his practical experience as a golf coach is a rare combination among today's golf instructors; however, these credentials will soon become the expected standard in years to come. The traditional fault-and-fixes golf lesson is rapidly being replaced by comprehensive, science-based coaching—the ultimate prescription to taking your game to the next level.

High Performance Golf identifies the scientifically-proven, tour-tested training strategies used by the game's elite players. You will learn how these champions utilize coaching, assess their skills, set goals, organize their schedules, conduct deliberate practice, choose equipment, stay fit and develop their mental toughness.

High Performance Golf provides you with a lifetime prescription for mastering the game of golf. No quick-fixes, no short-cuts to fame—just a realistic game plan for improving and maintaining the health of your golf game! All you need to do is read on, absorb the medicine, and then go out and apply it to your game. The only side effect—lower golf scores!

Acknowledgements

Special thanks are in order to the following people for their support and guidance with making this book a reality—Lorin Anderson, Beth Farrell, Dave Allen, Tara Gravel, Douglas Brunton and Willard Ellis.

INTRODUCTION

Golf is going through a fundamental shift at this point in its history. After a century-long hiatus, the sport will rejoin the Olympics as part of the 2016 Summer Games in Brazil. This is significant. Now more than 70 countries around the globe will focus on the sport like never before, looking to develop their best athletes for a run at the medal podium in Brazil and future Games. Millions of dollars are flowing down from government sport federations to establish a developmental infrastructure for golf. In addition, more sports science professionals are being recruited to turn their attention to golf. Biomechanists, physiologists, psychologists, motor learning scientists, and periodization planning specialists are now supporting coaches to enhance golfer performance. This approach has proven to be successful in all other Olympic sports—it's how world records fall with regularity—and there's no reason to think it won't have a similar impact on golf.

Now more than ever before, elite golfers and coaches are looking outside of the traditional golf instruction blueprint to the modern sports science world for key information on how to better develop skills in order to peak perform for competition. The book you're about to read explores many of these applications as well as other performance factors and how they influence results, including coaching, practice, mental-game preparation, periodization, game planning and strategy, club fitting, skills assessment and testing, and fitness. Most of today's young stars—among them Rory McIlroy, Yani Tseng, Jason Day, Rickie Fowler, Matteo Manassero and Ryo Ishikawa—are not accidental champions. They're exceptional athletes who have developed their skills and confidence with the advantage of assistance from coaches and sports science experts since their early exposure to the sport. They have reached the pinnacle of their sport at an earlier age than has ever been seen before. They are shining stars, and examples, in this new golf era.

High Performance Golf is a comprehensive book written for aspiring golfers interested in exploring all of the variables that influence development and performance. This book is a compilation of the experience that I have enjoyed as a PGA of Canada Master Professional and Canada's National Golf Coach for 13 years, along with the expertise and ideas graciously shared by so many of golf's top coaches and minds: Dr. Rick Jensen, Dr. John Marshall, Peter Sanders, Dr. Deborah Graham and Jon Stabler, Dr. Gary Wiren, Dr. Penny Werthner, Jim Ahern, Fred Shoemaker, Jim Fraser, Steve Ball, Dr. Paul Schempp, Frederik Tuxen, Dr. Tim Lee, Dr. Greg Rose, Dave Phillips, Todd Sones, Bob Vokey, Dr. Bob Christina, Dr. Greg Wells, Matt Frelich, Dr. Dana Sinclair, Greg Redman, Peter Mattson, Dr. Anders Ericsson, Dr. Jean Côté, Gary Bernard, Dr. Nick Martichenko, Paul Sherratt, Charlie King, Craig Shankland, Mike Bender, Pia Nilsson, Lynn Marriott, Eric Alpenfels, Rick Grayson, Michael Hebron, Peter Knight, Lynn Booth, Rudy Duran, Doug Roxburgh, Dr. Steve Norris, Dr. Ernst Zwick, Dr. Robert Yang and David Donatucci.

This book is intended for serious golfers interested in improving their performance and exploring their full potential. It is for aspiring juniors, collegiate players, touring professionals and all golfers who truly want to play their best and are committed to doing so irrespective of their handicap. This book is also an excellent resource for coaches, golf administrators and parents who support developing players, and need to be informed and aware of all that is involved.

High Performance Golf is aligned with the principles of Long-Term Athlete Development (LTAD)—the guiding light of all Olympic sports science experts. What makes this book a must-read is that it works! It's tried, tested and true. In my time as the Canadian National Coach, I have seen firsthand what can happen to athletes and coaches who understand and effectively apply this information. I have used the methods in this book to coach world-class performances at the junior, collegiate and elite amateur levels. These methods have produced National Champions, World Junior Champions, NCAA Champions, NCAA All-Americans and Player of the Year Award winners; one player even rose to No. 1 in the World Amateur Rankings. The best of the best have moved forward to succeed on the PGA and LPGA Tours.

Those who adapt these training techniques will likely see consistent improvement and remarkable results. *High Performance Golf* provides you with a proven pathway to performance excellence. I encourage you to use it to your full advantage.

Henry Brunton
July 2012

For my wife Rhonda and son Cole, I am blessed.
Thanks for your love and support!

1
BUILDING EXPERTISE:
HOW ELITE GOLFERS DEVELOP

*"You see kids specialize in golf. I think that's idiotic.
To play all sports is great. I played everything. I think
that kids should be playing everything, doing everything.
Eventually, if you want to specialize in something,
that's fine. But go out and enjoy, and be happy to play
other things."*

—Jack Nicklaus
Sports Illustrated Golfer of the Century

I interact with scores of outstanding young golfers who dream of one day becoming star junior players, decorated NCAA collegiate or elite amateur performers and, ultimately, world class touring professionals. They have clear goals and one final destination in mind—the PGA or LPGA Tour. This is critical to their development because if you can't dream it, you won't achieve it.

Surprisingly, however, few aspiring golf athletes and the people who support their efforts (i.e., parents and coaches) are aware of the principles of Long-Term Athletic Development (LTAD), including how long it takes to reach the world-class level and how much effort and commitment is required to get there. They're not certain what they should be doing at different ages and stages of development. Without this knowledge, many athletes, parents and coaches make decisions that are incongruent with what sports scientists recommend. Although well-intentioned, their efforts are relatively unproductive, and lead the athlete to inadvertently experience a plateau with their performance—or move farther from their goal.

This chapter is all about providing aspiring athletes, parents and coaches with a clear pathway of how world-class professional golfers develop. It draws on what sports science research information supports—how elite golfers effectively develop the expertise and confidence necessary to succeed at the highest levels of their sport. The information in this chapter will give you some guidance and benchmarks to use as measuring sticks to see how you stack up, and whether you're on track to realizing your full potential. Armed with this information, I'm confident you can work toward becoming the best golfer you can be.

THE TALENT ICEBERG

When people observe and applaud outstanding competitive golf performance, they're generally unaware of the many critical factors that contribute to this performance. The Talent Iceberg illustration pictured here shows the many influences going on beneath the surface—key variables that impact the development and competitive performance of an elite golfer. Created by Stuart Morgan of Golf England, the pyramid-shaped Talent Iceberg is a great resource for young golfers who want to know just what it takes to become one of the very best at their sport.

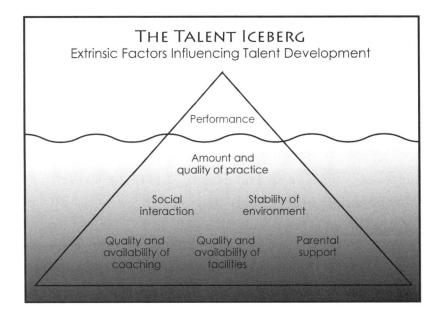

The Talent Iceberg
Extrinsic Factors Influencing Talent Development

Performance

Amount and
quality of practice

Social
interaction

Stability of
environment

Quality and
availability of
coaching

Quality and
availability of
facilities

Parental
support

Reaching the Pinnacle of the Sport

The English government-funded agency Sport England researched the career paths of dozens of golfers dating back to the Bobby Jones era, and found that the best male and female players took an average of 20 years from entry point (i.e., the time they first took up golf) to winning a major. The average starting age was 8.3 for males and 9.1 for females, and the average age of winning that first major was 31.3 for males and 25.6 for females. It takes about 20 years from the time these athletes begin their experience in golf to reach the point where they're in position to win major professional championships.

It's a Marathon, Not a Sprint!

It's common to encounter players, parents and coaches who believe that in order to one day play on the PGA or LPGA Tour, you must first be an accomplished junior champion. Research, however, indicates that *early winners are often not the winners in the end when it counts most*. It tells us that

3

more than 80 percent of teenage champions in all sports do not become adult champions. In fact, many child champions leave their sport before they reach adulthood. This is due to a variety of reasons, including burnout, boredom and injury, says Dr. Steve Norris, a world expert on Long-Term Athletic Development from the Canadian Sports Centre.

Childhood success is not a precursor to major championship success. I'll give you an example: The USGA Junior Amateur Championship is considered the most prestigious title in the world for golfers under the age of 18; the champions in this event have clearly established themselves as world-class players for their age group seemingly guaranteed to be on the Pro Tour in the future. But this just isn't so. As part of a research paper that I authored for the PGA of Canada in 2007, I discovered that in the 25-year period stretching from 1976 to 2000, 22 different U.S. Junior champions were crowned. (Tiger Woods won this event three consecutive times.) Of these 22 winners, only eight players eventually earned PGA Tour Cards (36%) at some point in their careers; and only four of these players were still members of the PGA Tour in 2007 (18%). They were Tiger Woods, David Duval, Brett Quigley and Hunter Mahan.

BE AWARE OF "OUTLIERS" (I.E., "FOOL'S GOLD")

If you're truly committed to exploring your potential as a high-performance golfer, take the time to understand the information presented in this chapter and throughout the book. There are definite patterns to how elite athletes develop. Be aware of what sports scientists say you should do and not do at each stage of development. Understand that these are very reliable fundamentals likely to give you the best chance at succeeding in the future.

Of course, there are exceptions to most every rule, i.e., players who made it to the top of their sport without following the typical developmental pattern. These people are called "outliers"—a friendly term recognizing that there is not just one way to succeed. Outliers are unique individuals who become successful even though they may "break the rules," or fail to follow the conventional patterns of those who normally make it to the top of their sport. Two-time major champion John Daly comes to mind quickly as an obvious outlier because he was able to reach superstar status despite his less-than-ideal personal life habits off the course. Tiger Woods, Rory McIlroy and Yani Tseng can also be considered outliers since they all won major professional championships at a younger age than what is considered normal and were significantly ahead of the developmental curve. Woods was 21 when he captured his first major, the Masters in 1997; McIlroy was 22 when he won the US Open in 2011; and Tseng was 19 when she won the LPGA Championship in 2008.

RID YOURSELF OF THE ENTITLEMENT ATTITUDE

Realize that a career as a world-class professional golfer is a phenomenal accomplishment, limited to a select few people worldwide. No one should feel entitled to ascend to this prestigious level just because they desire it. Oftentimes developing athletes expect to become top-level players because the lifestyle and status of a touring pro is so appealing. In many cases, parents also share this point of view, believing that their child is entitled to ascend to the highest levels of the sport. Rid yourself of this entitlement attitude if you have it because no one owes you anything in competitive golf. Focus on doing whatever it takes to earn your way to the top. Everyone playing professional golf has earned their way there, and they must keep on earning it to stay out on tour. There are no exceptions.

REALITY CHECK: NOT EVERYONE CAN MAKE IT TO THE BIG LEAGUES

The cold, harsh reality is that very few people will realize their dream of competing at the world-class touring professional level. The illustration below clearly shows that superior expert performance is uncommon and extraordinary.

10-YEAR/10,000-HOUR RULE

Olympic athletes and their coaches are aware of the "10-Year/10,000-Hour Rule" from the acclaimed research of Dr. Anders Ericsson of Florida State University. Ericsson, author of *The Road to Excellence*, has studied practice and performance in activities and professions from sports to medicine. He defines world-class experts as the top few hundred people in any activity, and his research shows that it takes about 10 years and more than 10,000 hours of practice to ascend to world-class levels of performance. Aspiring high-

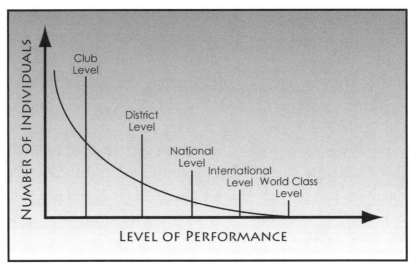

Ericsson, 1993

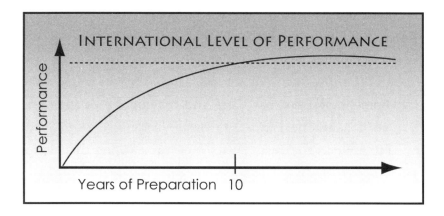

performance golfers need to be aware of this information and behave accordingly.

The findings of this research suggest:

- It takes at least 10,000 hours of deliberate practice over 10 years (or more) to attain international levels of expert performance.
- Most experts engage in deliberate practice for about 4-5 hours per day.
- Most individuals never achieve their potential because they do not practice optimally, i.e., they're not acquainted with highly refined, intense, deliberate practice.
- The evidence doesn't support the myth that hard work at the start will enable one to coast into future success.

CÔTÉ'S 3 STAGES OF DEVELOPMENT

Dr. Jean Côté, an internationally renowned sports science researcher and chairman of the School of Kinesiology and Physical Education at Queen's University in Canada, discovered

7

that there is a pattern to how elite athletes develop. He broke sports development into three stages for elite athletes: the Sampling Years (ages 6-12), the Specializing Years (ages 13-15), and the Investment Years (age 16+). The following is the development pattern that Côté and his colleagues found to be common amongst elite athletes. This information gives aspiring athletes the best possibilities for realizing their long-term full potential.

Stage 1: *The Sampling Years (Ages 6-12)*

Dr. Côté discovered that elite athletes typically try six to eight different sports/activities when they were 6 to 12 years old. At this age children should spend hundreds of hours playing informal neighborhood-type games to develop the ABC's of physical literacy—jumping, running, throwing, catching, balance, agility, and striking skills. These skills can be transferred to any chosen sport in the future. Kids should sample different sports of interest to see where their passion lies and move toward these activities as they mature. They should compete in a healthy way that is fun and inspiring, and leave the really serious competition until the later stages.

There should be minimal adult intervention at this classic outdoor play stage. The children should be left alone to use their creativity to modify the rules of the sport to suit the situation. They need to know only the basic fundamentals and general rules and need little structured practice led by coaches and parents. Any professional coaching should be conducted by a PGA Professional or expert who has specific training in programming and skills development for children who are in their sampling years.

Parents should value physical activity and sports participation, and let their kids know that what they're doing is a good thing. They should support their kids as best they can, and let them have fun since that's what this stage is all about.

Coaches should teach the basic fundamentals and rules of the sport in simple ways that the children can understand and apply. Safety is priority No. 1, but the kids should be allowed to play. Coaches should also play with the children if they can, creating child-appropriate hole lengths and scorecards, and competing with them in games and various contests. Activities should be fast-paced, incorporating fitness and movement-skill education. Provided the learning experience is fun, children will want to come back.

Stage 2: *The Specializing Years (Ages 13-15)*

In the development of elite athletes, an important transition occurs around age 13 with the start of high school. Elite athletes reduce their involvement in other sports, and begin to compete at the local or state/national level in their primary sport. Fun and enjoyment remain central elements, but the children choose to spend more time in deliberate practice, building the necessary skill and confidence to compete and excel under pressure. In all of the families studied by Côté, parents didn't pressure children to perform, but they did start helping them structure their deliberate practice (i.e., by setting up a fitness room at home or putting a synthetic putting green or hitting net in the backyard). The parents become involved in the children's activities without giving feedback or participating as a playing or training partner. Parents stop coaching their children and help them find a professional coach trained in helping competitive players develop. They also do their best to provide appropriate access to golf courses, practice facilities, equipment and competition.

The athlete starts to develop a closer relationship with his coach during this stage. At the same time, he should also:

- Make golf one of his top two sports.
- Start following periodized annual plans with help from his coach.
- Learn effective practice habits and training regimens.
- Dedicate equal amounts of time to deliberate play and deliberate practice.
- Measure and evaluate his improvement/performance in both training and competition to be sure that his practice efforts are effective.

Athletes competing in two sports should do so in opposing seasons so as to focus more intently on golf. It's recommended that they play 72-plus holes of golf per week for seven-plus months and practice deliberately (focus on skill development/ improvement) for 15-20 plus hours per week. There should be a three-month off-season, since rest and recovery are very important elements of elite-athlete development.

As players start to compete on the state/national level, coaches become more serious and technical. Ideally, these coaches should provide a holistic, multi-faceted training program that is in alignment with the principles of LTAD. The coach should involve other support personnel, too, to help with the athlete's physical and mental growth. Coaches should focus on developing solid fundamentals and technique but also teach the entire game, i.e., how to prepare, practice, and play under the Rules of Golf. Coaches should play with the players and watch them compete to observe their tendencies as well as provide feedback whenever possible. The coach should also have the necessary equipment and technology—TrackMan, ShotByShot.com, etc.—to serve these players for equipment fitting and skills/technique assessment. In addition, the coach should help the athlete create a formal goal-setting plan and competition schedule that is appropriate for the player given his age, skill, future goals and available resources.

Stage 3: *The Investment Years (Ages 16+)*

Côté found that elite athletes make another transition at about the age of 16. He coined the phrase, "The Investment Years," because at this stage athletes decide to make a full commitment to the sport in which they want to excel. They invest the vast majority of their time and energy in training and competing for this sport.

Athletes in this stage should focus on full-time training and competitive programs that will enable them to build skill and confidence in this sport. They should be aware of all aspects of elite performance—technique training, the mental game, fitness, nutrition, course management and game planning—and have specific strategies to improve at each. They should be very coachable and have the attitude of a champion people—they should see themselves moving to the top levels of the sport in the future, and be willing to pay the price.

The parents' investment in their child at this stage mainly involves financial support. The parents often have to make sacrifices to allow their children to have the best training and coaching available. They respond to the demands and expectations on their child by fostering an optimal learning environment and providing access to high-level coaching, rather than creating new demands or pressures. Parents fade into the background and become fans, staying out of the way of coaches and sports administrators.

At this stage, athletes need to be served by coaches who can provide an "Olympic-style" holistic coaching and training program. These coaches observe players in on-course training and competition, and create comprehensive annual plans for practicing and competing. They are fully committed to helping the athlete achieve his goals, and have a strong relationship with both the player and his family. The coach relies on a strong team of sports science experts—an Integrated Support Team (IST)—to give the athlete the best chance for long-term development and success.

THE TREE METAPHOR

VISION54 co-creators Pia Nilsson and Lynn Marriott, authors of *Every Shot Must Have a Purpose*, *The Game before the Game*, and *Play Your Best Golf Now* have had a profound influence on my coaching. They use The Tree Metaphor to give coaches, parents and athletes an excellent picture of how golfers develop most effectively.

The tree has three distinct parts—the branches, trunk and roots. Each part is unique but intertwined. The branches, the part we typically see the most of when we look at the tree, represent the outcome. In golf, everyone sees the outcome first, i.e., the scoreboard or scorecard. People look at the outcome and make judgments based on what they see.

The trunk is referred to as the intention. There is no growth in the branches if the trunk doesn't develop first. In addition, the outcome never changes if the intentions don't grow and develop first.

The roots of the tree are the most important part in terms of growth and survival, passing energy to the trunk and branches. The roots are underground and their importance and influence are hidden. A golfer's roots include swing fundamentals,

TRAINING DON'TS

Like any sport, there are pitfalls to avoid when considering a rigorous training program. They include:

- *Early specialization before the age of 13. This should be avoided at all costs as it can lead to burnout, avoidable overuse injuries and an early departure from the sport.*
- *Too much structure and formal competition before age 13.*
- *Parents coaching their children after age 10.*
- *Never taking a break from golf. All athletes need an "off-season" of at least three months per year.*
- *Overemphasis on results in the early stages of development; the focus should be on training and skill building.*
- *Being too serious in all three stages. It's okay to have a "game face," however, so smile and enjoy the sport as much as possible.*

nutrition and fitness, and personal relationships. They must all be strong for your tree to grow, and deep roots will help you withstand storms (i.e., slumps).

In order to grow into a big tree, it's important that your intentions are clear and that they're the focus of your attention. The first step is to determine whether you really want to be a big tree or top-level golfer. Is your intention clear? Are your commitment and behaviors aligned with your intentions? If so, as a sapling (junior golfer) you need to be nurtured with adequate water, sunshine, love, good soil and fertilizer. Your

THE TREE METAPHOR

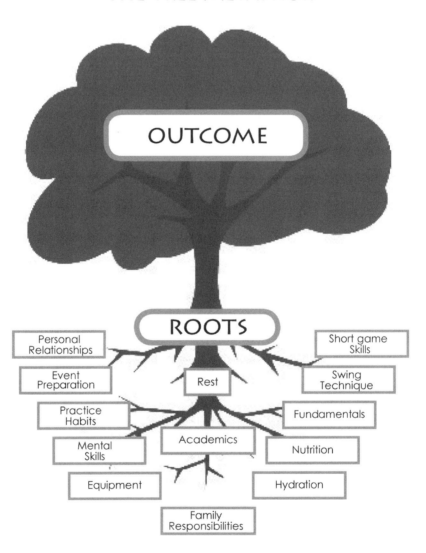

ONGOING FOCUS OF ATHLETE AND COACH

Develop strong and deep roots
to get improved results.

gardeners or caretakers (coaches and parents) need to keep a close eye on you. It's critical that they listen and talk to you, encourage you and pick out the weeds (i.e., discipline you when appropriate). Your tree needs a lot of time to grow and, at times, it will seem as if it isn't progressing at all.

As your tree ages and matures, it will need more space and less interaction by caretakers. It can almost look after itself. Great trees spawn other new baby trees (by mentoring younger junior golfers). They renew themselves through other trees, their genes passed on so that the game can continue to flourish.

2

CHOOSING A COACH

"Coaching is unleashing a person's potential to
maximize their own performance."

—John Whitmore

If you're reading this book, you're serious about taking your game to the next level, whether that means earning a spot on your high school team or playing NCAA collegiate golf. You likely have dreams of playing on the PGA or LPGA Tours someday. If you're a parent, you just want to know how to help your son or daughter achieve their dreams and make their experience as positive and fun as possible.

So what does it take to become an elite-level golfer? It requires skill, dedication, focus, hard work, top-notch competition, and good coaching. The latter is especially important. If it's your goal to become a PGA or LPGA Tour Professional, you will not get there on talent alone. In order to succeed on the next level (collegiate golf and beyond), you'll need a coach and other support personnel who can help you develop the necessary technical, physical, strategic and mental skills required to become an elite golfer.

This chapter is all about understanding how coaching works in golf—what it really is and what it isn't; what the differences are between a coach and an instructor; what you and your parents' roles will be in working with a coach; and how much you need to budget for coaching. You'll learn what specifically to look for in order to find the right coach for you. This is one of the biggest decisions that you'll make as an aspiring high-performance golfer. You'll want to get it right!

What Is a Golf Instructor?

He or she is typically an individual trained and certified by the PGA or LPGA to conduct effective golf lessons and group clinics. Golf instructors are very important people in the golf industry, because they're often the first point of contact for beginning golfers just coming into the game; they're also responsible for keeping these beginners interested when they struggle to make solid contact or become frustrated with the game. Golf instructors mainly concern themselves with helping golfers establish sound fundamentals (grip, posture, alignment, and ball position), swing mechanics and short-game skills. They help people learn the fundamentals of the game and give them the information and feedback necessary to play better golf.

What Is a Golf Coach?

A golf coach must be a golf instructor first. Just as a psychiatrist must first become a certified medical doctor before becoming a specialist, a golf coach must develop the fundamentals and technical skills necessary to teach golfers how to swing a club efficiently and play the game. However, a golf coach is also trained to teach aspiring golfers how to play the game better, i.e., put the ball in the hole as quickly as possible. They typically serve serious golfers who are more experienced and adept at the game. Golf coaches focus on a myriad of factors that influence the golfer's performance and results on the course. In addition, they focus on club fitting; effective practice strategies; skills assessment testing and evaluation; statistics collection and analysis; goal setting; on-course patterns and behavior; schedule planning; game-planning strategy and tactics; and so on. The most advanced golf coaches enlist other professional support personnel to assist them. They create and lead an Integrated Support Team (IST) that includes a sports medicine specialist, sports psychologist, strength trainer and nutritionist.

Golf coaches provide their athletes with "Olympic-style" holistic coaching and training. They observe their players on the course, both in training and competition, and assist these athletes in establishing comprehensive annual plans which detail all facets of training and competition throughout the year. They support in monitoring and modifying these plans as necessary. Coaches create a partnership with each player and stress the importance of academics and life planning outside of the sport. A good coach should involve parents, guardians, team coaches, and other support group personnel in the player's development, and teach players to respect and honor the game.

SELF-COACHING OPTIONS

If necessary, you can "self-coach" effectively to a point. There are some excellent books, DVDs, and developmental tools available online that provide the correct information and feedback you need. Two-time U.S. Open champion Retief Goosen learned how to play the game reading "how to" books, specifically Jack Nicklaus's *Golf My Way*. Hall of Famer Lee Trevino never had a golf lesson. It's not the preferred way, but there are a number of top pro players who have had to do it alone. It can be done.

WHEN TO SEEK OUT A COACH

Kids interested in playing golf will benefit from professional instruction and coaching from a PGA Professional as early as age four. LTAD compliant/age appropriate athlete development programs for youngsters interested in golf are becoming more and more commonplace. Before the age of nine, kids golf-development programs should be fast paced and dynamic—in alignment with the attention span and motivation for young people involved in sport—fun and exciting. These programs involve teaching basic golf fundamentals and ball-striking skills acquisition; however, they also teach movement skills known as the ABC's of physical literacy—jumping, throwing, balance, striking, agility and other physical skills. These skills can be transferred to all other sports. Early sport-specific specialization should be avoided at this stage, as it's likely to lead to burnout. There is plenty of time to get serious about the sport later.

From ages 9 till 12, it's advisable for parents to enroll their child in a golf-development coaching and training program provided they want to explore the idea of their child playing golf competitively. This type of program ideally offers regular private coaching on a one-on-one basis, along with weekly supervised group practice and play; kids also learn the rules of competition and are taught good sportsmanship.

If a child is committed to exploring their limits as a competitive golfer, they should reduce their involvement in other sports and begin to compete seriously at the city, state and national levels. This should occur at about the age of 13. What's more, if they show a keen interest in becoming an elite-level golfer, the parents should stop coaching them. Parents should introduce their child to a PGA Professional who is a trained "coaching specialist," and then get out of the way. This may be difficult for some but if you want to give your child the best chance to develop and succeed, back off from coaching and let the professional work his or her magic. The athlete should be training with the coach at least twice a week for about nine months per year.

FINDING THE RIGHT COACH FOR YOU

Identify potential coaching candidates through research and networking. Do a Google search to see who is in your area. Ask top players, their parents, and leading club professionals in the region whom they would recommend, or call your local PGA Section and State Golf Association and ask for a list of coaches who specialize in teaching competitive junior golfers. Call a coach's former players for references, if needed. A good coach should never motivate through fear, intimidation or shame, no matter what level of play is involved. Avoid these coaches, no matter how successful their record is.

If you're seeking the very best of the best, you can find a list of all current and former *GOLF Magazine* Top 100 Teachers at golf.com. *Golf Digest*'s list of America's 50 Greatest Teachers can also be found on their website, golfdigest.com, as well as a list of America's 50 Best Women Teachers and Top-20 Teachers Under 40. Log onto uskidsgolf.com to see the US Kids Golf Top 50 Kids Teachers and Master Kids Teachers.

Make a short list of potential candidates, and then contact them via e-mail or telephone to arrange a face-to-face meeting. You know you've found the right coach for you if:

- The coach has the necessary skill, experience, and proven track record to help you achieve your goals.

- You're confident that the coach can help you succeed.
- You feel comfortable working with him or her.
- The coach is genuinely interested in helping you.
- He or she has the time and energy to serve your best interests.
- The coach has the necessary facilities and technology to help you.
- He or she communicates effectively with parents, making them aware of common pitfalls that can hurt a golfer's success.
- You can afford to pay for his or her services.
- It "feels" right—you can see yourself enjoying your time with this coach.

BUDGETING FOR A COACH

Once you've made the decision to hire a coach, you'll need to establish a budget. Be honest about how much you can afford for coaching. Ideally, you would have the wherewithal to "do it all" with the coach of your choice, but if this is not possible, prioritize where you can get the biggest bang for your buck. If, for example, your fundamentals and swing mechanics are holding you back, then spend your coaching dollars on improving your technique. You may be forced to "go it alone" in other areas like mental training, fitness, and game strategy, if your budget doesn't permit you to be with a coach as much as you'd like. Do the most with the resources that you have available to you.

WHAT DOES COACHING COST?

It's unlikely a golfer can ascend to the highest levels of the sport without the guidance a coach provides. Highly trained coaches are in demand and charge fees that reflect their training, experience and professional standing. You can expect to pay $100 to $150-plus per hour for some of the top teaching professionals. Some offer a season-long comprehensive coaching program for a flat fee. A serious 9- to 12-year-old will need about 10 hours of formal instruction and coaching per month to develop his fundamentals, swing motion, short game, and basic course management. After the age of 13, a child who is serious about developing into a top-level competitive player needs at least 15-20 hours of coaching support per month. In general, you and your parents should budget between $3,000 and $10,000 annually for coaching fees. This may sound shocking to some; however, it is not out of line with what athletes in other high performance sports pay for expert coaching.

Parents need to be aware of all of the costs involved in playing competitive golf so that they can budget their money and time accordingly. Keep the cost of equipment and balls, membership/green fees, tournament registration fees, clothing and shoes, and travel and food costs in mind. In addition, competitive junior golfers need transportation and support in getting to and from training facilities and competitions.

What to Expect from a Coach

The relationship between coach and competitive junior golfer is far more complex than most people realize. When a good coach begins working with a new golfer, he or she should first assess the golfer's skill level and game then help the golfer establish a detailed, written strategy to improve. The coach will recognize strengths, benchmark them against players at the same development stage, and build upon them. The coach will also identify opportunities for enhanced performance then work with the player to turn these weaknesses into strengths in time. The player should take ownership of this plan, and then work together with the coach to follow the plan in order to achieve the objectives.

As the coach and the player work together on their plan, the coach should:

- Help the athlete identify his or her goals.
- Give the athlete a comprehensive physical screen, or assessment, to identify any body/motor function weaknesses or areas of concern.
- Teach strategy and tactics course and game management decision-making skills.
- Work with the athlete to monitor, measure and reset goals as necessary.
- Provide advice and strategies for improving— pinpoint specific skills to improve and design a strategy for each.
- Ensure that the golfer's equipment and ball is optimally fitted.

After development of the initial player assessment, the coach, player and parents should work together on a broader, long-term plan. As an ongoing component of development—in addition to the technical aspects of the game—a good coaching program should do the following:

- Teach the athlete how to practice effectively.
- Teach mental skills and strategies.
- Teach the rules of golf
- Teach competition skills—event preparation/game plans
- Provide detailed feedback on player development.

- Help formulate a detailed goal-setting program and training regimen.
- Help establish a balanced and challenging competitive schedule.
- Collect accurate data from competitive rounds.
- Teach proper nutrition and hydration.
- Help create a strength training and flexibility regimen.
- Communicate openly with the athlete, parents, golf officials and collegiate coaches.
- Encourage and nurture the athlete on and off the course, and help him understand who he is as an individual.
- Help the athlete plan for post-junior options.
- Continue to support an athlete after he or she retires or turns professional.

THE COMPETITOR'S ROLE AND RESPONSIBILITY TO THE COACH

Once you find the right coach, you and your parents will be spending a good deal of money to improve with his or her help. But, just as the coach has responsibilities to you, you have responsibilities to your coach. First, you have to be honest and have an open dialogue with your coach. Make the coach aware of anything that is unclear or unsettling. If you're unsure why he is prescribing a particular drill or practice regimen—or if you have doubts that it will help or you simply don't want to do it—then speak up and ask him about it. A coach appreciates this. He can explain things so that you're clear and buy into the idea, or he can present you with alternatives.

Additionally, while you're free to respectfully disagree with your coach from time to time, you need to be coachable,

SUCCESS STRATEGY FOR JIM SMITH
Prepared by Henry Brunton
Date: August 14, 20__

*Jim, the following feedback is intended to make
you aware of your strengths and to identify gaps or
opportunities for improvement so that you can progress
toward your long-term goals.*

*Please don't mistake any of my comments for
negative criticism. I believe in you whole-heartedly
and want to see you reach your full potential.
You're conducting yourself like an elite athlete. I'm
delighted and excited for your future. You can count
on my support all the way.*

Ultimate Goals
- *To win the U.S. Amateur*
- *To win an NCAA Championship*
- *To win the Ohio Am*
- *To become a member of the PGA Tour*

Strengths
- *Maturity/self-awareness/focus/desire and
  commitment. You're fully committed to "paying
  the price" that's required to make it to the big
  leagues.*
- *Fitness/conditioning. Continue to develop in this
  area.*
- *Ball speed/power. Testing shows that you are
  explosive through the hitting zone—160 mph of
  ball speed—close to the PGA Tour average.*
- *Scoring/playing instincts. You have excellent self-
  awareness of how you play best and score lowest.*

Gaps—Opportunities for Improved Performance

- *Fundamentals and swing technique. I will assist you with polishing your pre-swing fundamentals and swing so that you can have a more Tour-like ball flight and more "shots" in your repertoire.*
- *Putting. You generally have strong putting skills; however, you can lower your stroke average with more intense practice. Use The Putting Arc training aid for 30 minutes every day and practice putting for an additional 30 minutes daily.*
- *Strategy/tactics. I want you to establish written game plans, including targets and strategies for each hole. We'll also be playing to specific approach yardages throughout the season at your competitions.*
- *Equipment. It's imperative that we make sure all of your clubs are optimally fit.*

Summary

Jim, please accept my feedback as it's intended—to help you focus on specific behaviors and activities that will lead to improved performance. I really believe in you and your ability. I would love to see you succeed at the amateur level and beyond. I'll be in contact in the next few days to follow up.

i.e., you must be willing to do what's asked of you, even if it can be uncomfortable or frustrating at times. Improved results usually take time for high-performance athletes. When making changes, golfers often feel uncomfortable with the changes and take a step back before they move forward. Be patient. After all, you're establishing new habits and movement patterns. The brain and body need a lot of focused repetition to get in sync with one another. I often preface changes by saying, "You'll likely hate me for introducing these changes. It's going to be uncomfortable. But be committed to them. You'll be thankful that you did in the long term. It's short-term pain for long-term gain." You have to trust your coach; he or she knows what will most benefit your game in the long run.

You should follow "the plan" you've come up with together to the letter; practice and compete as recommended; pay the coach promptly; and "fire" the coach immediately if you become less than 100 percent committed or if you plan to go in a different direction. Conversely, be forewarned that your coach may "fire" you if you don't hold up to your commitments and obligations.

THE PARENTS' ROLE

While most of this book addresses the junior athlete, I'd like to talk directly to the athlete's parents as well. All parents play a pivotal role in their child's athletic development—after all, you're probably the people from whom he inherited his love of the game—but too often the line between parent and coach is blurred. In order to give your child the best chance to reach his or her potential, you should let a coach do his job without interfering. Your best role is that of non-judgmental cheerleader and appreciative spectator, someone who provides unconditional love regardless of your child's golf performance. You should do everything you can to avoid adding pressure to the challenges that tournament golf presents.

Ideally, you'll have a discussion with your child about how he or she wants you to act as a golf parent. Does he want you to walk along with him at tournaments, or to simply offer support after a round? Does he want to share every detail of his practices and competitive rounds, or periodically fill you in on the big picture?

To help your child get the most from his relationship with his coach, you should meet with the coach at the very beginning and periodically afterwards—both with and without your child—to discuss both your role and the coach's role and expectations. Make sure to establish open communication, and don't let any issues fester.

You'll also want to avoid the common pitfalls of parental behavior, which include:

- Living vicariously through your child. (Remember, he is playing, not you.)
- Coaching your child in golf. Athletes at this level need professional coaching, as well as parents who specialize in being mom and dad.
- Rewarding your child only when they're successful on the course. Your child needs encouragement and support most of all when he or she is down. He or she also needs to remain grounded when performing well.
- Viewing your child's identity solely as a "golfer." Golf is not who your child is, it's one of many things that he or she chooses to do.
- Judging the performance, commitment and ability of your child.
- Adding to the considerable challenge and pressure the game inherently provides.

If you do cross the boundaries listed above, you will do far more harm than good. You might affect your child's love of the game, or your child might wind up reacting poorly to pressure (from you or themselves). Worst case, they might ultimately suffer from burnout and leave the game entirely.

10 THINGS I WISH SOMEONE WOULD HAVE TOLD ME IN HIGH SCHOOL
By Paul DeCorso

Paul DeCorso is past president of Acushnet Canada and a graduate of Kent State University in Ohio where he was winner of the 1989 Jack Nicklaus Award for Academic Excellence. He decided to give up competitive golf for the business side after the 1989 NCAA Championship, which he lost by a narrow 20-stroke margin to Phil Mickelson! I asked him to speak to the juniors at one of our camps. Here's what he told them:

1. *If you want to play golf, then get out there and compete!*
2. *Get a coach if you can.*
3. *Follow your passion and trust your gut.*
4. *Go to a good school (not necessarily one in the South).*
5. *The golf industry provides opportunity for a great life: You'll rarely become a millionaire, but you'll always live like one.*
6. *If you want to be on the road to success, then go to school.*
7. *If you want a smoother road to success, then get better grades.*
8. *Hey mom and dad, life's path is not decided by age 18! (Hey kids, you better have a good clue by age 22).*
9. *Set realistic goals for your playing career.*
10. *Earn it. Nobody owes it to you.*

3

COLLEGE GOLF:
EVERYTHING YOU NEED TO KNOW

"College golf can be an exciting and enriching experience for those who regularly make the travel team and compete for the school. On the flip side, it can be a [very] negative experience for golfers who don't earn the opportunity to play for the school in tournaments. My advice: Make sure that you truly have the ability to play on the team of your choice. Be honest and realistic."

—John Brooks,
Former NCAA D-I Coach,
University of North Florida
President, rednumbersgolf.com

Playing collegiate golf in the United States presents an exciting possibility for thousands of outstanding young athletes around the globe. Opportunities exist at the NCAA Division I, II and III levels or at NAIA or NJCAA schools for qualified boys and girls from the competitive junior ranks. Participating athletes on the collegiate level get to enjoy the challenge of competing on a team in an organized system like no other while they earn a college degree. As an additional cherry on the top, many of these golfers receive scholarship funding. The cream of the crop earn a "full ride," with all expenses paid for tuition, books and room and board, as well as golf equipment, coaching, facility access, and travel expenses to competitions.

So just how does it really work? This chapter is all about understanding how the U.S. Collegiate Golf System functions—separating the reality from the fantasy—and how prospective candidates can prepare years in advance to be on track to realize this possibility. Use this information to your advantage. Seize the incredible opportunities that collegiate golf presents if you are interested in this level of competition.

Choosing a college is one of the biggest decisions that a person will make in his or her life, and not because of the opportunity to compete on a golf course. Studies show that the quality of your post-secondary education and training directly correlates to your future income, where you'll live, whom you'll marry, the vehicle you'll drive and, ultimately, your quality of life. This decision is about much more than your future in golf—it is about your future. Period! Playing on a collegiate golf team may be important to you now; however, realize that committing to a college is about far more than the golf team. Be informed. Find the best opportunity for you as a person in the long-term, not just as an athlete in the short-term. Choose your colors wisely—be proud to be part of the school and what it represents on and off the course. I always advise college-bound athletes to imagine themselves at the school of their choice if golf is not part of their experience there. A person who is confident that their school of choice is right for them with or without golf is making a sound life decision.

WHY DOES COLLEGE GOLF EXIST?

Keep in mind that universities are in the business of developing people—educating and preparing students for future

NCAA MEN'S GOLF

Programs	Number of teams
Division 1	290
Division 2	199
Division 3	270
NAIA	172
NJCAA	193

Total number of teams: 1,124
Total number of golfers: 12,364

NCAA WOMEN'S GOLF

Programs	Number of teams
Division 1	256
Division 2	140
Division 3	131
NAIA	166
NJCAA	92

Total number of teams: 785
Total number of golfers: 5495

success in the real world. They're not institutions mandated to train and develop professional golfers. The reason why college golf exists is to provide talented individuals with a passion for their sport to continue to do so while concurrently combining these skills with academic and social development.

HOW BIG IS COLLEGE GOLF?

There are about 12,000 men and 5,500 women who compete in intercollegiate golf at the NCAA Division I, II and III levels and with the National Association of Intercollegiate Athletics (NAIA) and National Junior College Athletic Association

(NJCAA). NCAA divisions are determined by the number of students enrolled in each school, with the largest and best-known colleges and universities ranked as Division I.

How Many High School Golfers Advance to the Intercollegiate Level?

Very few high school basketball players in the U.S. get to play at the collegiate level, and the same holds true for high school golfers. About six percent of competitive high school male golfers play in a post-secondary program at a junior college or university, and less than two percent advance to the NCAA Division I level.

What Does It Really Take to Become a Collegiate Golfer?

Just as a university has academic minimum requirements, you should be prepared for minimum skill requirements as a golfer. The minimum standard for men is a 5 handicap in competition and a proven ability to post scores consistently under 76 in high school/junior golf competitions. There are a small number of players on many college golf teams that do not play to this standard; however, they seldom get off the bench or make the travel team. In order to have any reasonable probability of receiving scholarship funding assistance, you'll need to prove that you can perform at a 0 handicap level or better in top level junior golf events. The NCAA Division I powerhouse squads like Georgia, Oklahoma State and Stanford, scour the globe to recruit the world's best talent. They look for top-ranked American Junior Golf Association (AJGA) players who are +3 handicaps or better and who can play at the international amateur level with stroke averages lower than 72.

ALLOWABLE NUMBER OF GOLF SCHOLARSHIPS

Association	Men	Women
NCAA Division I	4.5	6.0
NCAA Division II	3.6	5.4
NCAA Division III	None	None
NAIA	5	5
NJCAA Division I	8 full	8 full*
NJCAA Division II	8 partial	8 partial*
NJCAA Division III	None	None*

*All women's NJCAA teams compete at Division I

Courtesy of Peter Knight

Don't get fooled by the "box scores" of collegiate events, which sometimes make players look like they are just good high school players. The length of the courses (generally 7,100-plus yards), hole locations and severity of the rough are significantly more difficult than what is typical in junior golf. As a result, top collegiate golfers are better prepared to have success on the professional level—often, more sooner than later. Consider: In 2011, two University of Georgia golfers, Harris English and Russell Henley, won professional events on the Nationwide Tour.

In addition to being able to shoot low scores on college-length courses, coaches for NCAA men's programs are looking for recruits with skills such as:

- Sound pre-swing fundamentals (i.e., grip, stance, ball position, posture and alignment).
- Golf swing patterns that enable them to control the direction, trajectory and spin of the ball.

- Sufficient power to compete on college-length courses—the minimum standard is 150 mph of ball speed and a carry distance of about 240 yards (with a driver); the average player on an elite men's D-I program has 165 mph of ball speed and 265+ yards of carry.
- The ability to control their emotions and stay calm under competitive pressure.
- Short-game skills that enable them to score consistently under 75 on championship courses.
- Consistent pre-shot routines.

Coaches are also looking for off-course skills such as:

- The ability to map a course and game plan for a competition.
- A good working knowledge of the Rules of Golf and the Rules of Amateur Status.
- A positive attitude and respect for the game, coaches and fellow competitors.
- Positive family support. Coaches don't want to deal with parents who are too overbearing or influential in the athlete's performance.

For women, competition for athletic scholarships is not as intense because there are fewer qualified players vying for scholarship dollars. That being said, there's a common misconception that virtually any woman who wants a golf scholarship can get one—this is not true. The elite NCAA women's programs recruit around the world for the best players. The top 50 NCAA women's programs look for players who have 2 handicaps or better. In general, a woman needs to be a competent and experienced competitor who can play to a 10 handicap or better in order to be considered for a golf scholarship at any level of collegiate women's golf. They need to carry their drives 175-plus yards with a ball speed of 115 mph. The top NCAA players carry their tee shots 225 yards or more and have ball speeds of 135-plus mph.

If you're currently a strong junior golfer and considering playing intercollegiate golf in the future, you can get a head start right now by developing into the type of player a coach would want on his or her team. If possible, hire a PGA Professional who has specialized training and expertise as a coach for developing elite junior players. Ideally, you'll have appropriate coaching support throughout your development. In addition, you'll need to:

- Gain considerable experience as a competitive golfer by playing a full schedule and challenging yourself against the best players in the highest-level events possible.
- Practice and train for 2-4 hours per day in addition to playing.
- Play 4-6 rounds per week.
- Make certain that your club/shaft/ball combination is optimized. Get a custom club fitting that uses launch monitor technology.
- Commit to golf-specific fitness and strength training.
- Learn and apply mental-game and self-management skills. Expose yourself to key information presented throughout this book.

WHAT ARE GOLF SCHOLARSHIPS?
Golf scholarships should be viewed as financial assistance

grants. They're awarded by college institutions to players who've earned them based on athletic merit (performance and potential). These scholarships are the primary recruiting tool coaches use to attract top players to play for their squad. If you're selected by the institution, and satisfy their academic entrance requirements (along with the NCAA's), you can be awarded a golf scholarship.

Fully funded NCAA Division I men's golf programs dole out a maximum of four and a half scholarships among their 10-12 players. A full ride is rare and limited to the very best golfers. NCAA men's D-II programs have three and a half scholarships maximum to disperse. Fully funded NCAA D-I women's golf programs have as many as six scholarships to grant per team, while women's D-II teams have four and a half scholarships maximum to hand out. Each college golf team generally has 8-12 players per squad, but only five make the traveling team for each tournament. Division III men's and women's programs do not offer any athletic scholarships. In reality, thousands of college golfers receive no scholarship money.

How Do Academic Scholarships Differ?

If you're a high achieving student, you should research available academic scholarship possibilities and apply for any for which you may receive consideration. Academic scholarship funding can be awarded in conjunction with athletic scholarship awards.

What Is the NCAA Clearinghouse?

The NCAA Clearinghouse is a security branch of the NCAA. The purpose of the NCAA Clearinghouse is to screen potential student-athletes in order to determine that they meet eligibility criteria requirements, i.e., to ensure that they're not professional athletes and verify that they've satisfied the basic prerequisite high school required courses and SAT test score minimums. Prospective student-athletes are required to register online with the Clearinghouse, fill out a questionnaire and submit high school transcripts and college test score information. When an individual has been approved by the NCAA Clearinghouse, they're issued a number which must be submitted to college coaches to prove that they're eligible for official visits and college entry status.

What is "Amateur Status?"

Golfers must maintain their amateur status in order to be eligible to compete in collegiate golf. The United States Golf Association (USGA)—the governing body of golf—has clear rules on amateur status and what constitutes being a professional. A golfer has amateur status unless they've declared themselves a professional by entering a professional event as such (you have to check a box declaring so on the event registration form), or as soon as they accept compensation— money or its equivalent—for competing, giving instruction, or using their golf reputation or skill for personal gain. In short, in order to maintain your amateur status, do not under any circumstances accept prize money at a golf event, get paid for giving lessons or clinics, advertise for a business (print or TV ads), or be involved in any personal appearances associated with a commercial component. If in doubt, contact your state golf association or the USGA.

The Odds of Playing PGA Tour Golf

The cold, hard reality is that precious few NCAA players make it to the PGA or LPGA Tour. The average NCAA D-I men's program can expect one player to reach the PGA Tour every 24 years. For many schools, the next player to graduate to the PGA Tour will be the first. Far less than one percent of collegiate golfers will ever realize a career on the PGA Tour. The odds are just as sobering on the female side.

Many are called to pro golf, but few are chosen. Go for it with your full intensity if this is your dream—after all, some will make it to the top. However, be realistic in your pursuit: Prepare for life outside of tour golf, because even those that do make it will experience life as a "civilian" at some point.

CLIMBING THE LADDER FROM JUNIOR GOLF TO THE PGA TOUR

How do most PGA Tour players get where they are? They typically climb the ladder of success from high school and junior golf (state golf association competitions, and AJGA and USGA tournaments) to the NCAA, to elite amateur golf (U.S. Amateur and other elite amateur events like the Northeast Am, Porter Cup, Western Am and Southern Am), and then on to professional golf (the mini- and developmental tours such as the E Golf Tour and Hooters Tour) before ascending via PGA Qualifying School to the Nationwide Tour and finally the PGA Tour. Research shows that PGA Tour Players typically turn professional at 22.2 years of age and make it to the PGA Tour at 26.8 years old. Very few skip grades—77% of PGA Tour Players have won at least one event on the Nationwide Tour.

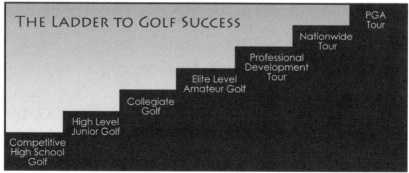

THE LADDER TO GOLF SUCCESS

PGA Tour
Nationwide Tour
Professional Development Tour
Elite Level Amateur Golf
Collegiate Golf
High Level Junior Golf
Competitive High School Golf

How to Market Yourself to a College

Marketing is creating demand for your service. In this case, the service is your ability to perform as a high-level golfer and student at the collegiate level. Like any goal, getting into the college or university of your choice is one you have to work toward (at least two years before you intend to enroll). You need to build a resume as both a student and an athlete that shows you have the skills, background and track record to succeed both on and off the golf course. Contact prospective college coaches by phone and email as early as your sophomore year in high school so that you'll be familiar to them. NCAA rules permit coaches to respond to your correspondence; however, they cannot initiate contact or officially recruit a player until July 1st of a player's junior year of high school. You're likely to hear a lot of "no's" before you hear a "yes" from a coach who is interested in having you on his or her team, so be persistent. Be business-like in your approach to the recruiting process by following up with regular emails and taking notes. Finding a school that wants you can be a long and arduous process. To start with, you'll need three key components to get a coach's attention:

1. *Resume*

Coaches usually request a detailed golf resume from prospective athletes. List your best tournament results and highest junior ranking, as well as any other achievements on the course. Also include your GPA, SAT scores and NCAA Clearinghouse number, if possible. Avoid cluttering your resume with irrelevant data, and make sure to read it over several times for accuracy and grammar. Coaches want to see that you put time into your resume. A good playing resume is succinct and well-formatted.

SAMPLE PLAYER'S RESUME

Jim Smith
122 Tiny Beaches Rd.
Bright's Cove, IN, 41441
(601) 123-4567
jsmith@gmail.com

Birthdate: April 1, 1994
Social Security Number: 000-000-000
Height: 5'10" Weight: 149 lbs
Name of School: Riverdale Secondary
Graduation Date: June 20__
GPA: 3.7

Other sports: Basketball and tennis
Extracurricular activities: Student Council

Competition Results and Highlights
2009 *(first year for golf competitions)*
Pepsi Tour Events
> *1st place, 13- to 14-year-old division at Wild Woods GC*
> *2nd place, 13- to 14-year-old division at High River GC*

2010
State Events
Indiana Amateur Championship
> *June 4: T3, Indiana Amateur Qualifying, shot 74 at Wolf Mountain GC*
> *July 10-13: T49, Indiana Amateur Championship at Riverbend GC*
> *Scores: 75-76-80-78 (youngest player to make the cut)*
> *Indiana Junior Match Play Championship (July 31-August 3)*
> *Qualifying Round: Placed 3rd, shot 70 at Brooksville GC*

First round: Defeated Bill Jones (25), 2&1
Second round: Defeated Fred Robertson (8), 4&2
Third round: Defeated by Ralph Freedman (9), 2&1

Pepsi Tour Events

1st place (three-way playoff), Junior Division, shot 74 at Wolf Mountain GC

Other Accomplishments

1st place in Men's Club Championship at Wild Woods GC, 74-68-79—221 (Note: 68 was shot in heavy rain)
1st Place in Junior Club Championship at Wild Woods GC

2011

Pepsi Tour Events

1st place overall at Rock Springs GC, shot 67
2nd place overall at Rolling Green GC, shot 70

State Events

Indiana Junior Tournament of Champions
May 5: T2, shot 73 in qualifying round at Mountainview GC
May 18-20: Finished T28 at Black Bear GC (80-80-82; all three rounds played in severe wind and rain)
Indiana Men's Champion of Champions
June 10: T16, shot 75 at Wild Meadows GC
Indiana Junior Championship
July 2: T4, shot 74 in qualifying round
July 16-19: T28 at Municipal GC (75-73-74-79—301)
USGA Junior Championship, Blind River, WA
July 19-23: T81, shot rounds of 75-77 at Irish Hills GC

Other Accomplishments

1st place overall (73), 2008 Black Brook GC Invitational, Salt River, IN

SAMPLE COVER LETTER

October 3, 20__

Coach Mike Jones
Head Golf Coach
University of Big Sky

Dear Mr. Jones,

Hello, my name is Jim Smith. I'm writing to you on the recommendation of my golf coach, Bill Jeffrey, a GOLF Magazine Top 100 Teacher. Coach Jeffrey raves about your program and your school's academic reputation and, after conducting some research of my own, I find myself equally impressed. I only recently started to put together a list of schools I'd like to attend in the fall of 20__, and the University of Big Sky has vaulted to the top of my list.

I'm currently a junior at Riverdale Secondary School in Bright's Cove, Indiana where I'll graduate in June 20__. As one of the state's rising junior golfers, I plan to play a number of high-level tournaments this upcoming season, including the U.S. Junior Amateur, Indiana Men's Amateur and Indiana Open, as well as several AJGA events. In 2009, I was the youngest player to make the cut in the Indiana Amateur, and in 2008 posted a first and second on the Pepsi Tour. My current handicap is 0, and I hope to lower it even further in the upcoming season.

I'm just as proud of my academic performance (3.7 GPA) as I am my golf achievements, and would like

to attend a school with a top-notch business program as well as a highly competitive golf team. I have a strong commitment to excellence and a passion to compete and excel at the NCAA D-I level, and am confident I have what it takes to be successful as a collegiate student-athlete. Please see my attached playing resume.

Coach Jones, I'm excited about discussing the possibility of joining your team and becoming a "Bronco" in the future. I can be reached at the email address and phone number listed below. Coach Jeffrey would also be glad to answer any questions you may have about me; he can be contacted at 601-932-6375 or via email at bill@billjeffrey.com. In the meantime, any information about your school and golf program that you could send me would be greatly appreciated.

Thank you for your time and consideration. I look forward to hearing from you in the near future.

Sincerely,

Jim Smith
(601)221-1235
jsmith@gmail.com

---

2. Cover Letter

Attach a cover letter to your resume, using the letter to introduce yourself to the coach. Explain briefly who you are, what kind of player and student you are, and your reason for getting in touch. Be organized and specific. Tell the coach why he should consider you as a potential student-athlete, and ask for a reply

45

back with information about both the school and the team. Include your email address and phone number. Make sure that your letter is not too long or cluttered with unnecessary information. Double-check your spelling and grammar. Don't send a form letter. Address the coach by name and refer to the program by its nickname where appropriate.

3. Reference Letter

It's a good idea to send prospective coaches a reference letter from someone who knows you and can speak with credibility about you and your golf ability. Avoid "nice" letters from high school teachers or friends of the family if possible. Instead, get a letter from an expert—ideally a PGA Professional or a current or former top-level college player—who can attest to your abilities and say that you have what it takes to succeed at the collegiate level.

PUT YOUR SWING ON VIDEO

Not all college coaches have the time or budget to watch those players they're actively recruiting in competition; instead, they rely on recommendations from current players, alumni and PGA Professionals. NCAA rules prohibit coaches from having you audition or try out for their squad if you visit their school. They're not permitted to tee it up with you on your visit nor watch you play. Because of these restrictions, most coaches will want to see a swing video of you, along with your cover letter and resume. Your coach or PGA Professional can help you with this. Be sure to get a close-up picture of your grip, along with action sequences of you hitting a driver, mid-iron and wedge from both face-on and down-the-line angles. There's no need for audio. And don't stress about the quality or be too particular. The coach simply wants to see your swing fundamentals and technique. You can either email the video, post it on youtube.com or burn it onto a CD and mail it.

WHAT TO KNOW ABOUT RECRUITING SERVICES

Recruiting services can help guide athletes and families through the recruiting process. Many do an excellent job; however, they're not absolutely necessary. Most charge between $1,000 and $2,500 (or more) to help market you to schools and coaches. They will polish your resume and cover letter, post your profile and upload your swing video on their website. There are no guarantees they'll secure you an official visit or an offer, however, and many coaches look unfavorably upon them. If you elect to hire a recruiting service, make certain that they are experienced experts in college golf who have a positive reputation with coaches and families who have been down this road before you. Do your homework before committing.

WHAT TO EXPECT IN THE INTERVIEW PROCESS

Aspiring collegiate golfers may encounter a wide array of recruiting experiences, depending on their standing and reputation. Highly recruited blue-chip prospects—players with a national/international following—are likely to have a much different experience than outstanding junior golfers who have strong regional records but are relative unknowns on the national scene. The latter group will be searching for a college program to embrace them and give them a chance to play. Junior golfers are likely to fall into three different categories.

1. *Top National/International Blue-Chip NCAA Prospects*

Blue-chip prospects are players ranked in the Top 100 of their respective birth year. They're known to virtually all college coaches, and have been scouted and courted by coaches who attend top junior/amateur events in the hopes of one day signing them to a scholarship. When these players are eligible to talk to NCAA coaches, they can expect to be invited on an official visit and get the rock-star treatment during their recruiting process.

NCAA rules allow 48-hour visits at up to five schools. Each school pays for travel, accommodations and other expenses incurred by the athlete, as governed by the NCAA. On these official visits, the prospective athlete will meet the coaching staff and current players, tour athletic and academic facilities, meet academic advisors, and perhaps play the home course (coaches are not permitted to watch). These visits are often organized around a major sporting event at the school, i.e., a football or basketball game, to give the recruit a feel for the culture of the institution.

At the conclusion of this visit, blue-chip prospects can expect coaches to make them a verbal offer of a significant scholarship—possibly up to 75 percent or more, depending on the player's ranking/status. NCAA rules preclude anyone from officially signing an agreement until the designated "Early Signing Period," which usually starts around November 1st of their senior year in high school. Players in this group can also expect a promise of playing time and other attractive incentives, within NCAA rules, to entice them to sign. NCAA rules prohibit schools from offering cars, cash or other perks to prospective recruits they hope to sign.

Sometimes it's the little things that make a player choose their college destination. One of my students, a Top 10 college prospect, made the maximum five official visits to elite NCAA golf programs, and shared his decision-making process with me. One of the deciding factors with his school of choice was the fact the coaching staff took the initiative to engrave his name on a brass locker plate before his visit. The coach said, "This is where you'll dress and come to play every day. We'll see you here." This seemingly small gesture got him very excited and proved to be a tipping point in his decision. He went on to enjoy a sensational collegiate career with this school that included an NCAA Team National Championship; he was also named an All-American his junior and senior seasons. Top programs will do everything they can within the rules to attract and sign the very best players.

2. *Outstanding State-Level Junior Golfers*

Precious few juniors get the opportunity to experience the rock-star treatment when being recruited; however, some high-potential athletes do experience a scaled down version. If you're a top-ranked regional/state high school player you're likely to be invited for official campus visits to two or three schools and receive scholarship offers of 25-60 percent or more. It's also likely you'll draw attention from coaches of those schools within 300 miles of your home. They'll follow and watch potential recruits in regional/state events and form relationships with local players as the rules permit.

3. *Other Outstanding Junior Golfers*

There are many junior golfers who are legitimate college recruits but don't fall in the two categories above. Junior golfers develop at different rates and not all college players were junior golf stars. Players in this category have to recruit the school rather than the other way around. Players in this category need to:

- Identify schools that are realistic for them; programs that are willing to give them a chance.

- Petition coaches and campaign for an opportunity by sending letters, swing videos and playing resumes.
- Arrange for unofficial visits if they attract interest from a school, and pay for their own expenses.

Following the visit and courting period, if there's mutual interest, the player may be offered a spot on the team—usually as a walk-on—and 0-30% in scholarship money. Players in this category shouldn't be discouraged. You can get to the top by beginning at the bottom.

One of my former players was, at best, just above-average as a senior in high school. He played to about a 5 handicap with modest results in state junior events, but had a strong desire to achieve and a lot of self-belief. He spent a good deal of effort recruiting schools that would give him the opportunity to play. He heard a lot of "no's" before he found a coach and a school to finally say "yes" and allow him to play as a walk-on. It wasn't a glamorous program—in fact, when he began his college career the team was ranked 267th in NCAA D-I—but it provided him with an opportunity to prove himself.

He made the most of his opportunity, recording a stroke average of 76.5 his freshman year while playing in roughly two-thirds of the team's events. He improved considerably in the next three years, developing into the school's all-time best player, winning three events and being recognized as their conference's Player of the Year. He received progressively more scholarship assistance, eventually earning a full-ride as a senior. After graduation, this player turned professional. He has played in two U.S. Opens and is now a regular on the Nationwide Tour. He may be the first player in this school's history to make it to the PGA Tour. Everyone develops at different rates.

A Typical Day for a College Golfer

NCAA golfers typically attend classes in the morning, have lunch, and then head to the golf course to train and play until dark. They miss a lot of classes to compete. Each team is permitted to play in competition for 24 to 27 days, in addition to conference, regional and national championship competitions. Players who make the travel squad will be on the road for more than 30 days per year.

Time-management skills and solid study habits are the only way for the student-athlete to succeed off the course. These schedules typically demand a general course of study instead of a more specialized field. It's hard for athletes to pursue high-level NCAA golf as well as specialized degree programs such as pre-medicine, engineering, or journalism.

Scholarships and Tuition

Most top-ranked junior golfers can anticipate about a 50-percent scholarship if recruited. Therefore, depending on the school, they might need to pay approximately $8,500 to $18,000 annually out of pocket. Due to the tremendous time demands on NCAA athletes, it often takes more than four years to graduate, so it's not uncommon for athletes to accumulate $45,000 to $90,000 in loan debt to earn a four-year college degree. This is a significant financial commitment that not every athlete/family is prepared to make.

What Happens When You Get An Offer

If you've been offered a spot on a college golf team, you'll likely be notified either by a phone call or an email from the coach. The first thing you need to do is make sure you understand the offer in its entirety. Ask for a detailed written breakdown of how much scholarship money you'll be receiving and how much you'll have to pay to attend the school. Ask about any hidden costs, such as whether you'll need a car. Inquire about academic aid if you qualify. All NCAA athletes and their parents/guardians sign a written agreement (National Letter of Intent) and fax it to the school to make things official.

Don't expect much instruction from your college coach when you do arrive on campus, as he'll be expecting you to show up game-ready. Not all U.S. collegiate programs have professional level coaches and many are led by sports administrators. You'll probably be practicing unsupervised at times or with minimal intervention, so you should be mature enough to practice effectively on your own. You'll also want to retain your own coach. Most college coaches expect this and embrace it.

TURNING PRO AFTER HIGH SCHOOL

College golf is not the only pathway to world class pro golf. In 2011, five of the Top 10 players in the World Rankings did not play NCAA golf—Rory McIlroy, Martin Kaymer, Lee Westwood, Charl Schwartzel and Jason Day. On the ladies side, Yani Tseng, Paula Creamer, Cristie Kerr, Suzann Pettersen and Morgan Pressel are just a few of the many world-class players who jumped to the professional ranks without playing in NCAA programs. This trend is growing, some say because of the academic rigors that NCAA programs thrust upon the student-athlete. It's difficult for many to find sufficient time and energy to balance the academic demands, training and competition, and thus reach their potential. Adam Scott left UNLV after one semester saying that college did not provide him with the time he needed to reach his goals and potential.

If you've thought about taking a similar route, be fore-warned: It's extremely rare for any top high school golfer to advance directly to the professional ranks, just as it is for a high schooler to make the jump to the Major Leagues in baseball. The odds of going straight from high school to the PGA Tour is about 0.0001% (substantially less than an NCAA graduate). If you choose this path, be sure to prepare an exit strategy—a meaningful plan that might include college or training for another career if things don't work out as planned.

If you're serious about turning professional right out of high school, you should be aware of the skill level you'll need to achieve. You should be able to play competitive golf at a +2 handicap level, regularly break par on championship layouts, and have considerable potential to improve. Dr. Rick Jensen, a renowned sports psychologist from Boca Raton, Florida, whose clients have won 33 major championships, advises players to enter PGA Tour Qualifying School only when they're able to maintain a stroke average lower than 70 for a full year on one of the professional developmental tours.

Professional golf is unique in that there are no general managers, transactions or teams. No one can cut you, trade you, or make you play out of position. On the flip side, developing

---

LONG ODDS

Even if you get into a top-tier program, know that fewer than one percent of all NCAA Division I golfers ever realize a career on the PGA Tour. In 2011, Ben Martin (Clemson) and Joseph Bramlett (Stanford) were the only two collegiate golfers from a pool of approximately 750 NCAA Division I and 3,100 total graduating male seniors who earned a PGA Tour Card in their first year out of school. Both failed to earn enough money as rookies to retain their PGA Tour Cards.

---

players have to pay for their experience. Typically, no one will coach, manage or guide you unless you pay for their services. These players typically spend $75,000 to $100,000 or more per year for living expenses, tour school expenses, event entry fees, coaching fees (coach/psychologist/personal trainer), caddy and cart fees, travel costs, golf facility fees, etc.

Chances are that even if everything falls into place, it'll take you years to become successful. A research paper that that I authored in 2007 showed that the average PGA Tour player turned pro at 22.3 years old and earned his Tour Card at 26.8 years old—an average of 4.5 years. (Go to *henrybrunton.com* to download this paper for free.)

4

REACHING YOUR POTENTIAL
SETTING CLEAR GOALS

"The greatest sports champions and business leaders are also the best goal setters. For ambitious people determined to make steady progress against their most significant aspirations, goal setting is an essential cornerstone in this process."

—James Citrin, Best-selling Author, Leadership Expert

It's imperative to set clear goals if you're truly committed to exploring your potential as a competitive golfer. Setting clear goals in a professional fashion can channel your effort and focus your energy directly toward your stated objectives. Research clearly shows that embracing and employing a formal goal-setting plan makes you significantly more likely to achieve your dreams.

While it may seem trivial and somewhat insignificant, goal setting is one of the key behaviors that separates the good golfers from the elite ones. I strongly encourage you to take the time to establish a goal-setting plan. In this chapter, I'll show you the power of formulating SMART goals so that you can effectively set them for yourself.

CHAMPIONS AND GOAL SETTING

"If you don't know where you're going, you might wind up someplace else." —Yogi Berra

Goals really work! GolfPsych's Dr. Deborah Graham and Jon Stabler, authors of The Eight Traits of Champion Golfers, *have counseled dozens of touring professionals, including major championship winners. Graham and Stabler teach their clients that goal setting:*

- *Increases levels of performance by an average of 16 percent*
- *Improves the quality of your practice and play by replacing boredom with new challenges*
- *Helps you replace fear and tension with focus*
- *Helps sustain motivation during slumps, injuries and long road trips, as well as the course of a long career*
- *Boosts self-confidence*

Everyone has goals. The highest achievers are the ones most likely to write their goals down and devise a systematic plan to achieve them. Many successful athletes have learned to tap into the power of formal goal setting by making their goals SMART: Specific, Measurable, Adjustable, Realistic and Time-based. In order for your goals to be SMART, you need to make them:

Specific: Are your goals clear?

Measurable: Can you objectively prove that you've met your goals?

Adjustable: If you achieve your goals sooner than

anticipated, can you increase the intensity of your goals? Or, if they become impossible, can they be scaled down to become more achievable?

Realistic: Do you truly believe that you can achieve these goals?

Time-Based: Have you set a date by which you expect to meet your goals?

An example of a SMART goal is "to lower my handicap index from 3.5 to 1.0 by August 15th of this year." This goal is SMART because it's: 1) specific by stating exactly what it is you want to achieve; 2) measurable since it can be calculated objectively using the USGA Handicapping System; 3) adjustable because it can be re-set as necessary; 4) realistic given your current skill level and your commitment to following an organized program that includes training, coaching, competition and evaluation; and 5) time-based since it states a specific deadline.

Remember when setting your SMART goals to state them positively. For example, rather than establishing a negative goal of "Stop missing greens from the fairway with my wedges," create a positive SMART goal, i.e., "Hit 70% of my greens in regulation from 70 to 100 yards in competitive rounds this year."

The following is an example of a Goal Plan for a high performance golfer. This is a very basic plan—a minimum expectation for any serious competitive player:

Season Goal Plan for Earl Thompson

- Lower competition handicap from 3.5 to 1.0 or better by August 15.
- Break par for 18 holes in a competitive round by September 15.
- Shoot 147 or better in a 36-hole competition.

- Average 2.5 birdies per round for the competitive season, which ends September 15.
- Average 10 Greens in Regulation (GIR) for the competitive season.
- Average 9 Fairways in Regulation (FIR) for the competitive season.
- Record at least one hole-in-one before season's end.
- Break 70 on my home course, Shadow Ridge GC, from the championship tees before September 15.
- Increase ball speed with driver from 151 mph to 155 mph by August 15.

Setting formal goals takes vision and drive. Just as an architect puts in the thought and effort required to draft a blueprint for a building, you'll be doing the same to create a blueprint for your golf and personal development. The following Performance Plan is an example of a very detailed and comprehensive success strategy. Follow the six steps outlined to draft your own blueprint, utilizing the accompanying worksheets. (Ideally, this should be drafted with the assistance of a coach.) You'll see for yourself the advantage goal setting gives to the highest achievers. It provides the focus and structure needed to turn dreams into reality:

SAMPLE PERFORMANCE PLAN
Prepared for: Jim Smith
Prepared by: Henry Brunton, *GOLF Magazine* Top 100 Teacher
Date: January 15, 20__

Jim, your "Performance Plan" is a cornerstone to success. It will focus your energy toward your objectives, as well as lead to enhanced performance and enjoyment. It will help us create and implement strategies for your training, education, coaching, and performance. We will utilize this plan continuously over the course of the year, so please make certain that it reflects precisely what you desire. This year promises to be an exciting one for you, and I look forward to helping you achieve your goals.

2011 Performance Review

Congratulations on all of your accomplishments for the year, the most significant of which I've highlighted below:

- Reduced your handicap from 3 to 1.
- Improved your competitive stroke average from 78 to 75.
- Lowered your short game handicap from 5 to 2.
- Recorded a career-low round of 67 at White Creek Golf Club.
- Qualified and made the cut at the Ohio State Junior Championship.
- Won the White Creek Golf Club Championship.
- On target to become a successful national-level competitor.

PERFORMANCE PLAN OBJECTIVE

The objective of the Performance Plan is to guide your development as a person and an athlete. Pursuing your goals in a professional and systematic fashion, as outlined in this plan, will help you attain excellence in all areas of your life.

Outcome Goals for the Season

1. Lower your handicap to +1 by June 30.
1. Lower your competitive stroke average to 73.5 for the season.

2. Lower your short game handicap to +1 by July 15.

3. Defend your White Creek Men's Club Championship title.

4. Finish in the Top 10 in the State Junior Championship.

5. Qualify for U.S. Junior Amateur Championship and make the cut.

Physical Performance Goals for the Season

1. Make certain that your set-up fundamentals and swing technique are sound.

2. Establish a "pro tempo" for all full shots and swing to 80 percent of your maximum power.

3. Develop a better short game handicap (+1 or better) using Short Game Test.

4. Hit more greens in regulation (10 or more on average for 18 holes).

5. Improve your accuracy off the tee (9 fairways hit per round on average).

6. Position your eyes slightly inside the ball when putting.

Strategies for Achieving Your Physical Performance Goals

1. To make certain that your set-up fundamentals and swing technique are sound, you will:

   • Work with your coach to review pre-swing fundamentals.

   • Use video to obtain feedback regarding swing technique.

   • Utilize a set-up "work station" to ensure that your pre-swing fundamentals are being correctly ingrained during practice.

2. To establish a "pro tempo" and learn to swing to 80 percent of your maximum power, you will:
   - Obtain feedback on tempo and swing speed from coach and video.
   - Train with speed drills during each practice session.
3. To develop a better short game, you will:
   - Make certain that all wedge lie angles and lofts are correctly tuned.
   - Work with your coach to review short-game technique.
   - Practice diligently to groove touch and feel as well as trajectory control.
   - Measure short game skill using Short Game Skills Test
4. To hit more greens in regulation, you will:
   - Employ better course-management strategies so that more fairways are hit in regulation.
   - Learn exactly how far each iron carries and rolls.
   - Devise effective game plans with a focus on hitting a higher percentage of GIR.
   - Chart performance using post-round reports and a ShotByShot.com stats program.
   - Practice diligently with short irons.
5. To improve accuracy off the tee, you will:
   - Make sure the equipment and ball you're using fit (use TrackMan to verify).
   - Learn to swing within yourself (80 percent of maximum power) on all tee shots.
   - Employ sound pre-swing fundamentals, especially alignment.
   - Practice tee shots diligently (1 hour per day with focus).

- Establish a game plan for each tee shot with an emphasis on club selection.

6. To get your eyes in position slightly inside the ball when putting, you will:
   - Review putting fundamentals with your coach.
   - Obtain feedback on form from your coach.
   - Use putting mirror training aid to develop proper eye position over the ball.

Mental Performance Goals

1. Be calm and in control mentally and emotionally on the first tee.
2. Clearly "see" the target before 80 percent or more of your shots.
3. Use a simple mental routine before every shot.
4. Regulate thoughts between shots 95 percent of the time.
5. Create swing keys that focus on rhythm, tempo and the target.
6. Focus on "right brain" creative non-technique thoughts. Get away from thinking "technique." Instead, imagine where you want the ball to go and let the magic happen.
7. "Feel" your swing, its tempo and rhythm.
8. Focus on hitting your ball toward your intended target without any conscious thoughts of technique ("hold the angle," "release the hands," "complete your backswing," etc.) while you're trying to execute.

Strategies for Achieving Your Mental Goals

1. To remain calm and in control on the first tee, you will:

- Use relaxation techniques to control tension in the body and quiet the mind (i.e., breathe deeply "in and out" through an imaginary straw).
- Monitor and maintain emotional composure on the golf course as much as possible.

2. In order to envision your target before 80 percent of your shots, you will:
    - Learn visualization techniques and apply them. For example, focus on the target for four seconds before returning your eyes to the ball, and then immediately "pull the trigger," maintaining the image of the target in your mind's eye.
    - Practice these skills using a "Mental Game Practice Scorecard."
    - Transfer these skills to the golf course.
    - Use post-round reports to monitor your progress.

3. To establish a simple mental routine before every shot, you will:
    - Work with your coach to develop mental routine training.
    - Practice these techniques to ingrain your routine and make it automatic.
    - Make the routine part of your practice regimen.
    - Use a Mental Game Practice Scorecard to help you transfer your routine to the golf course and competitive situations.
    - Use post-round reports to monitor your progress.

4. To regulate your thoughts between shots 95 percent of the time, you will:
    - Work with your coach to learn about "thought control" concepts and principles.
    - Practice these skills until they become habit.
    - Learn how to relax and distract yourself.
    - Recognize unwanted thoughts and get rid of them.
    - Use post-round reports to monitor your progress.

5. To create swing keys that focus on rhythm, tempo and the target, you will:
    - Work with your coach to learn an effective mental pre-shot routine: "See it, feel it, strike it."
    - Learn to play without conscious thought; react to your targets and the imagined flight of the ball.
    - Practice using cues and thoughts that improve your rhythm and tempo.
    - Use post-round reports to monitor your performance and progress in this area.

Life-Balance Goals

It's important to set "time-management" goals to ensure that you have sufficient energy and "inventory" (time) to make your life fun and rewarding. This will help you to achieve your goals as a student, athlete, son, sibling and friend. Set your life up so that you can have fun and be as challenged as you choose. Spend quality time with your parents and siblings in activities that don't necessarily reflect your personal interests.

In a typical week, based on eight hours of sleep per day, you might want to spend your time like this:

Academics (38 hours)	34%
Golf (30 hours)	27%
Meals and miscellaneous (20 hours)	18%
Dating (6 hours)	5.5%
Personal (hobbies, relaxation) (6 hours)	5.5%
Family (5 hours)	4%
Friends/social time (7 hours)	6%

Non-Negotiables

1. Do your best.
2. Have a positive attitude.
3. Respect others.
4. Take full responsibility for all of your actions.
5. See poor rounds and mistakes as opportunities for growth.
6. Be honest with your coach and yourself.
7. Complete ShotByShot.com stats after each round.

Tournament Schedule

1. Draft a preliminary season event schedule.
2. Remember to respect the training, competition and reflection cycle as much as possible.
3. Work with your coach in the coming weeks to finalize your schedule, which will be approved by your parents.

Post-Secondary Education Plans

1. You're planning on enrolling in college in August of next year.

BECOMING A CHAMPION

James Citrin, a best-selling author and expert in personal growth and transformation, interviewed extraordinary people such as Arnold Palmer, Colin Powell, Lance Armstrong, Mia Hamm and Tony Hawk for his book The Dynamic Path *(2007) in which he says:*

"Becoming a champion is grounded in trusting that your aspirations merit significance and that you have the capacity and potential to reach your goals. You must believe that you are investing your life in something worthwhile and that you have a legitimate chance of making it happen."

2. You're committed to identifying the best possible institution that enables you to continue your development as a young man and an athlete.
3. You're going to research 10-15 possible schools.
4. Go for it! Your coach will support you as much as possible.

STEP 1: *Set Outcome Goals*

The first step in goal setting is to look at the big picture and establish your outcome goals. Setting your sights on an ultimate destination will help you plan your trip there.

Outcome goals summarize where you want to be after a certain amount of time—usually a year. Setting your goals one year ahead keeps them somewhat distant but not so far off that they're inconceivable. If you like to motivate yourself well into the future, you can also set some longer term goals

WORKSHEET #1
My Yearly Outcome Goals:

_____

_____

_____

_____

_____

just as Tiger Woods did when he set the goal of topping Jack Nicklaus's record of 18 major wins. Olympic athletes do this: They plan for the next Summer or Winter Olympic Games, which can be as much as four years away. Outcome goals are *measurable results or outcomes*, such as finishing in the top 10 of the Order of Merit, being selected for a team, getting your Tour Card, etc.

Once you've determined where you want to be in a year, post the goals somewhere visible. Don't bury them in a file in your computer. Do what Tiger Woods did, for example, and tape them to your bedroom wall or bathroom mirror for daily reflection.

While you'll want to be reminded daily of your long-term goals, they need to be kept away from the course. Focusing on outcome goals during play or practice can negatively impact your performance and development. To play your best in competition, your mind must be in the present.

STEP 2: *Identify Your Physical Performance Goals*
Physical goals help you practice and train with a purpose,

and lead to improved skills and better competitive performance. They get you to focus on your fundamentals, technique, shot execution, and game management so that you can accomplish your outcome goals.

Some examples of Physical Performance Goals would be:

- To lower your short-game handicap to 2 or better by the midpoint of the season and to 0 or better by the middle of August.
- To learn how to hit a knockdown shot and use it successfully in competition.
- To improve your clubface position at the top of the swing.
- To keep your front wrist bowed when chipping.

STEP 3: *Outline Your Strategy for Achieving Your Physical Performance Goals*

Setting your Physical Performance Goals will allow you to plan a strategy for improvement. For example, once you set a goal of hitting an average of nine fairways in

---

WORKSHEET #2
Physical Performance Goals:

_____

_____

_____

_____

_____

---

regulation per round for the following season, your strategy can include:

- Optimizing your equipment; meet with a trained PGA Professional to see that you're using the right head, shaft and ball combination so that your driver is properly fitted to you.
- Working with your coach to ensure that your fundamentals and technique are sound.
- Practicing tee shots one hour a day, four times a week with targets and pylons set up to form a 30-yard wide fairway.
- Evaluating your skill proficiency weekly; hit 30 drives in practice to see what percentage of tee shots finish in the makeshift 30-yard-wide fairway.
- Recording the number of fairways in regulation that you hit in practice rounds and competitive rounds.

Follow this pattern with each of your Physical Performance Goals, keeping in mind the business world mantra, "What gets measured gets done."

WORKSHEET #3
Explain your strategy for achieving each Physical Performance Goal:

_____

_____

_____

_____

_____

STEP 4: *Establish Your Mental Performance Goals*

Ask top amateurs and professionals how big a role the mental side plays in tournament golf and virtually all will answer 80 percent or more. In other words, once a player has developed the necessary fundamentals, swing technique and ball-control skills necessary to compete in tournament golf at a high level, their performance is still largely contingent on how they control their internal state—thoughts, focus, tension level and emotions. You may not be comfortable with this aspect of the game, but don't be intimidated. Commit yourself to learning mental-game skills, and take responsibility for practicing them just as you practice swing technique. Work with a coach to get feedback and to stay on track. Once you're informed and are comfortable with mental game skills, you are ready to set specific goals and appropriate strategies for achieving them.

Mental performance goals describe the mental skills—from attitude to self-talk—that you will identify and commit to strengthening in order to achieve your outcome goals. Mental performance goals should be your primary focus during competition. They include things such as:

- Establishing a thorough written game plan for every competitive round.
- Using deep breathing and other relaxation techniques to diffuse pressure and lower tension.
- Staying emotionally neutral during play—not reacting to poor shots or bad breaks by displaying your frustration.
- Talking to yourself in an encouraging and positive way—be your own best caddy!
- Following your mental pre-shot routine at least

WORKSHEET #4
Mental Performance Goals Worksheet:

_____

_____

_____

_____

_____

90 percent of the time—"See it, feel it, strike it." [Please note: I say 90 percent because it's impossible for most humans to be perfect with their thought control and focus 100 percent of the time.]

STEP 5: *Outline Your Strategy for Achieving Your Mental Performance Goals*

Just as you did with your physical performance goals, you should plan out how to execute your mental performance goals. Some of the things you may want to focus on include:

- Establish a written game plan for each competitive round.
- Be your own best caddy at all times—talk positively to yourself, be encouraging, believe in yourself, and make smart game-management decisions.
- Stick to your mental routine as often as possible; keep score of this.
- Give yourself a "point" when you focus on your target, the feel of your swing, and the desired flight of your ball immediately before hitting the shot.

WORKSHEET #5

Explain your strategy for achieving each Mental Performance Goal:

_____

_____

_____

_____

_____

STEP 6: *Life-Balance Goals*

Golf is a game that demands intense focus and discipline to ascend to the highest levels. There's no question that it takes an incredible amount of time and channeled effort to develop into a top-level competitor. Getting to the pinnacle of competitive golf is no different than journeying to the top of Mount Everest: You won't ascend to the top level without extraordinary commitment and sacrifice. Some talented athletes expect to ascend quickly in their sport because they want to and feel entitled to do so. Don't "expect" to be an outstanding competitive golfer. This won't happen. As I say to my players, "The only place that success comes before work is in the dictionary."

However, there is a tipping point. Many golfers become too focused—they're raging to master the game to the point of their own detriment. All they want to do is play golf, practice golf and watch Golf Channel. This behavior can negatively impact their game and their life. Catch yourself if you fall into this trap because to play your best and live life to the fullest, you must realize that your social life, academics, friendships

WORKSHEET #6
Your Personal Balance Goals:

ACTIVITY	HOURS/WEEK	% OF TIME
School	_____	_____
Work	_____	_____
Golf	_____	_____
Relationship	_____	_____
Personal Time	_____	_____
Family	_____	_____
Friends/Social	_____	_____

and the time you spend with your family can all impact your game and vice versa. Good balance in all areas of your life enhances your health, happiness and success.

Good balance for aspiring competitive golfers in this sense is different than it may be for others that are not endeavoring to explore their limits in a sport or activity. Here are some suggestions regarding "balance" for serious developing competitive golfers:

- You're strongly encouraged to make academics your top priority—go to class and study. Good habits in the classroom are likely to transfer to the golf course and vice-versa.
- Put full energy into developing your golf skills, body and mind with the goal of improving your performance. Make certain that you're spending your energy efficiently. Follow the guidance of your coach.

- Have a social life and a life outside of golf; however, don't let it be a detriment to your studies and your development.
- Make time for your family—you'll never regret it.
- Factoring in eight hours of sleep each day, you have about 112 waking hours to spend every week. The following worksheet will help you quantify the percentage of time that you plan to devote to practice and competition, as well as your family, friends, school, etc.

Academics (38 hours)	34%
Golf (30 hours)	27%
Meals and miscellaneous (20 hours)	18%
Dating (6 hours)	5.5%
Personal (hobbies, relaxation) (6 hours)	5.5%
Family (5 hours)	4%
Friends/social time (7 hours)	6%

How Your Coach Can Help You Realize Your Goals

In this example, Jim has clearly set SMART goals with the assistance of his coach. The player should make changes until it reflects his or her wishes. The player now "owns" this plan and can work together with the coach toward achieving the goals. This is fun and exciting for the player and the coach. It's professional and organized and leads to improvement and results.

5

PERIODIZATION: PLANNING FOR PEAK PERFORMANCE

"The superior man respectfully appreciates the cycles of increase and decrease."

—I Ching

Periodization is the concept of dividing an athlete's training into various parts—or periods—over the course of the year, with the goal being to facilitate both skill development and peak performance. The idea is to get the athlete to peak (i.e., play his or her best) for the most important competitions of the year.

In the 1970s and '80s sports scientists from the former Soviet Union and other Eastern Block countries used periodization as a foundation to train and develop champion athletes. Periodization training is now used by virtually all Olympic athletes and top performers around the world. It's a key principle in modern applied sports science in the advancement of training, coaching, competition and rest patterns. Understand it and use it to your advantage.

In this chapter, you'll learn how to apply the principles of periodization as it pertains to the sport of golf. You'll learn how to create your own Periodized Annual Plan and also learn how to plan an effective tournament schedule that is appropriate given your age, skill level and goals.

CREATING AN ANNUAL PLAN

A Periodized Annual Plan helps you systematically break down the year into phases in order to structure your training, coaching and competition effectively, so that you can develop skill and confidence to play your best when it matters most. An Annual Plan also helps you to avoid injuries and burnout. If you're a competitive golfer in U.S., it's recommended that you divide the calendar into the following four phases:

PHASE 1: Pre-Competitive (January 1-April 14)
PHASE 2: Competitive (April 15-September 15)
PHASE 3: Post-Competitive (September 16-October 31)
PHASE 4: Off-Season (November 1-December 31)

These starting and ending dates are flexible and can be adapted to different countries and climates. For example, Australian golfers play their summer events in December and January so their Post-Competitive phase is likely to fall when most golfers in the northern hemisphere are getting ready for competitive golf. Junior golfers in the U.S. compete primarily from mid-April through mid-September.

You're strongly encouraged to work with your coach to chart out a Periodized Annual Plan with specific training and development activities for each different phase. This plan should match up with your goals. Commit to following it. Executing a plan like this gives you a significant edge on your competition and gives the best chance at performing your best at key events. Note that this is a basic Periodized Annual Plan.

Periodization:
The Concept and Practical Application

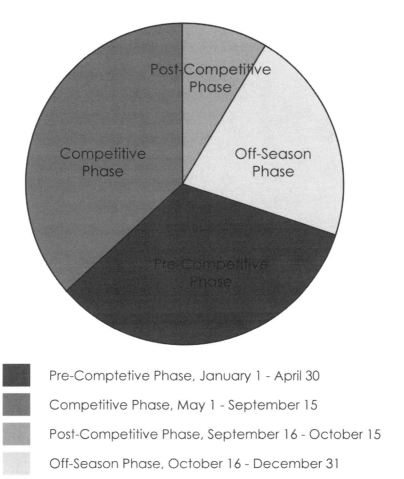

Pre-Comptetive Phase, January 1 - April 30

Competitive Phase, May 1 - September 15

Post-Competitive Phase, September 16 - October 15

Off-Season Phase, October 16 - December 31

Most elite golf athletes take this planning to the next level, as they chart out what they plan to do on a monthly, weekly and daily basis.

PHASE 1: *Pre-Competitive (January 1-April 14)*

The Pre-Competitive season is the time of year to get your body, mind, fundamentals, technique and equipment in shape for the golf that really counts—the competitive tournament season. The golfer in this phase is like the farmer in springtime preparing his fields and planting his crops for a fall harvest. The old saying that "You reap what you sow" certainly applies here, because the more effort you put in during this phase, the better results you can expect during the competitive season. The following areas deserve the most attention in this phase:

Equipment: Work with your coach to check all of your equipment, including your bag, shoes and rain gear. Inspect your clubs for damage such as dents in shafts, loose weights and worn grips. Also note significant changes to your body, swing or fitness level that may affect the optimal length of your clubs, grip size or shaft choice. Review your set makeup: Do you need new irons? Wedges? A new driver? Is your ball still the best choice for your game? Make the necessary repairs or adjustments and purchase any new clubs that you need, within your budget.

Planning/Administration: Work with your coach to complete your written goal-setting and Performance Plan. Draft a competitive schedule then submit entry forms for your events as soon as possible. Determine how much coaching you'll need and then schedule your sessions. Formulate a budget and make sure to monitor it throughout the year. Make special arrangements for school and work if you need to be excused in order to compete.

Health and Fitness: See a sports physiotherapist for a comprehensive screen to be sure that there are no preventable or underlying physical issues that may affect your swing or cause injuries in the long-term. Follow a customized golf-specific fitness and strength training program. (You can visit the Titleist Performance Institute website at mytpi.com for more information and guidance.) Make sure to work on your endurance (cardiovascular), strength and flexibility. Evaluate your nutrition and hydration habits and create a plan to follow while training and on the course. You should also have your vision checked by an optometrist. Lastly, be sure you're getting at least seven hours of sleep a night.

Skill Development/Practice: Begin to hit balls on the range, chips and putts to get the rust off. Have a session or two with your coach to review and reinforce pre-swing fundamentals (grip, posture, ball position and alignment), swing technique and short-game skills. Begin a practice regimen to improve your putting, short-game and full-swing skills, not to mention your pre-shot and post-shot routines. Meet with your coach for regular training and skill development sessions, as planned. Play outdoors in a non-competitive environment. This is "discovery golf"—playing without expectations in a stress-free environment. Discovery golf helps you become aware of your strengths and weaknesses, as well as those skills you have full or very little confidence in. Plan a training week in a warm climate during spring break if possible to play "discovery golf."

Mental-Game Skills: Make a list of books to read for awareness and skill development. Recommended reading might include: *Every Shot Must Have a Purpose* by Pia Nilsson and Lynn Marriott; *Extraordinary Golf* by Fred Shoemaker; *The Little Red Book* by Harvey Penick; *Golf is Not a Game of Perfect* by Bob Rotella; *The Inner Game of Golf* by W. Timothy Gallwey; and *How Great Golfers Think* by Bob Skura. Among the better CDs on this subject are *Golf Mind*, from the Subconscious Training Corporation, and *Train Your Golf Brain* by Dr. Karl Morris.

Additional Pre-Competitive Phase Activities: Intensify training as the competitive season approaches. Test to determine exact carry yardages for all clubs, being alert for any redundant clubs or large yardage "gaps."

PHASE 2: *Competitive Season (April 15-September 15)*

The Competitive phase of the season is the time of year when a golfer shifts into performance mode and away from a skills/swing development mode. Now it's time to put faith in your training. It's important to maintain any gains you've made whether physical, mental or with your technique or equipment. It's also important to commit to event preparation and daily practice. Collect performance data (catalogue and learn from it) and try and spot any significant trends. The golfer in this phase should be fully committed to shooting the best scores possible. The following areas should be addressed during this phase:

Equipment: Work with your coach to test all of your equipment in an outdoor setting. Use TrackMan or similar launch-monitor technology to evaluate clubhead and ball speed, spin rate, dispersion patterns, trajectory, carry distance and other relevant ball flight data. Be sure that all of your equipment fits and is in good condition, and be prepared to make any necessary adjustments. Monitor lies and lofts of your irons every other month, and check the wear patterns on your wedges. Replace them as necessary.

Planning/Administration: Review and reflect with your coach on your written goal-setting and Performance Plan and make any necessary changes. Finalize your competitive schedule, and re-confirm that your registration information has been received for all events. Monitor your budget and check that you're operating in accordance with it.

Health and Fitness: Continue to do your planned fitness workouts, combining both cardio and strength training. Consider visiting the mytpi.com website regularly and having those workouts e-mailed to you. Make sure to stretch before and after each training and playing session, and stay properly hydrated and nourished. Try and get at least seven hours of sleep per night and continue to follow your on-season nutrition plan. Never abuse alcohol or drugs.

Skill Development/Practice: Follow a detailed skill development/practice regimen designed by you and your coach. Make notes after each practice session and share them with your coach. Play at least nine holes a day five days (or more) per week, weather permitting, and use the Red Zone Short Game Skills Test (see page 152) to evaluate your proficiency in all facets of the short game. You can administer and score it yourself.

This test serves as an excellent evaluation/motivational tool that directs and focuses practice. Keep an up-to-date and accurate USGA handicap, which is an excellent barometer of skill and potential.

Mental-Game Skills: Review the mental-game books you read during Phase 1. Listen to mental game CD's for 10 minutes a day, three times per week, and reflect daily on your outcome and process goals. Collect mental-skills evaluations of all competitive rounds.

Stats Analysis: Collect accurate statistics on all key facets of the game using the personalized online program at ShotByShot.com, or a similar service. (ShotByShot.com is an online skills collection and evaluation program that I use with all of the players on the Canadian National Teams. It takes approximately 6-8 minutes to input your key statistics and provides immediate, useful feedback. (See page 152 for more information on ShotByShot.com.)

Miscellaneous: Pursue other activities to provide a break from golf and to stay fresh. Take at least half a day off per week to go to a movie or relax with friends and family. Leave your clubs at home!

Event Preparation: Prepare like a pro for competition: Research the weather and dress for it, and learn as much as you can about how to play the course beforehand. Host clubs usually have detailed websites illustrating the holes and how to best play them. If they don't, talk to the host professional and his staff; they'll pass along useful tips about the course and all of its nuances. Prepare game plans and course maps using YardCard (yardcard.com), an 18-hole course template used by many top competitive players and college teams. With YardCard, you can draw the holes, record yardages, make notes and prepare a written game plan, all of which you take with you to the course. Use distance gauging devices whenever possible in practice and competition. With handheld GPS devices like SkyCaddie, the course is mapped for you; there's no need to do the work yourself. The technology also enables you to gauge and chart how far your shots are flying and rolling on the course. Bushnell laser rangefinders and other similar devices are tremendous tools for measuring yardages. (Both USGA-approved GPS and laser technology can be used in some competitions at the discretion of the Rules Committee.)

Don't forget to research the practice/warm-up facilities where you'll be competing: Know when you can use them, or whether there are more suitable options close by. Visualize playing the course the best way that you can the night before the competition. Finally, plan to arrive at the golf course one to one and a half hours before your tee time to follow your normal warm-up routine.

PHASE 3: *Post-Competitive Season* ### *(September 16-October 31)*

The Post-Competitive season is an important phase in the calendar year that is commonly overlooked and misunderstood. Your actions in this phase play a pivotal role in your development and performance during the competitive season to follow next year. Although the golf season isn't over, it's time to take a breather from high stress golf, relax, and play for fun. However, there's still some work to be done: Players are encouraged to reflect on what's going well and what could be better. It's also time to begin planning and strategizing for next season: You and your coach should evaluate your progress in all facets of the game, paying close attention to your performance trends. Here are a few other things to assess during this phase:

Equipment: Think about whether you want to make changes for the following year. This is a good time to test new equipment, whether it be a driver, a long iron replacement (i.e., hybrid) or a putter. Examine your records and determine whether the changes you made (to your equipment) for the competitive season were useful. Make a list of what you need to repair or replace for next season.

Planning/Administration: Assess your tournament schedule and formulate a tentative plan for next year. Examine your budget and compare your planned budget with what you actually spent.

Health and Fitness: Continue your fitness and nutrition regimen to maintain your fitness levels. If you have a nagging injury, now is the time to address it: Work with your doctor or physical therapist and devise a plan to rest and rehabilitate the injury. Spice up your workouts by introducing some new exercises to your routine. Try a new sport or activity that combines mental and physical exercise, like yoga or a tai-chi.

Skill Development/Practice: Reflect on the competitive season: What went well? What could've been better? How could it have been better? Evaluate your coaching support, your statistics, and your competitive results. Refocus your goals and begin to work on any necessary changes to your fundamentals or swing mechanics: Are there any specific parts of your game (i.e., bunker play, chipping, putting, etc.) that need attention? Play for fun and taper practice to about two times per week.

Mental-Game Skills: Reflect on your goals daily. Continue to read and expand your off-the-course knowledge, but pursue non-golf activities and interests.

PHASE 4: *Off-Season (November 1- December 31)*

All athletes need an off-season, and golfers are no different. The off-season is an important time for you to recuperate physically, mentally and emotionally. Don't fall into the trap of believing that you'll accelerate your development if you continue to play and train intensely—or worse, believing that you'll fall behind if you take any time off. This leads to burnout and avoidable injuries. To perform your best the next season, it's crucial to take time away from golf, otherwise you're likely to experience boredom, fatigue and complacency. Give yourself permission to take a break during this period, because it will keep you sharp, motivated and excited to play next year.

Your off-season objective should be to work diligently on a golf-specific fitness and strength training program. While you want to give your body and mind the opportunity to breathe and regenerate for the ensuing year, you can still get much stronger physically. It's an ideal period to focus on your fitness and academics, and to spend more time with friends and family during the holiday season.

PEAK PERFORMANCE: PREPARING FOR YOUR MAJORS

Touring professionals prepare meticulously for every event in which they compete. They do their best to ensure that they are "ready" to play their best on the first tee come Thursday. Some pros, like Tiger Woods and Phil Mickelson, make an even bigger push to peak at the biggest events, i.e., the four major championships. They think about these events months in advance, often making a special trip or two to play and scout the venue. Woods has been known to take the week off prior to majors. He'll practice and train with a vigilant focus on the course he'll be playing the following week, hitting the shots he feels he'll need to compete and win. During this time, he'll do his best to simulate the course and weather conditions that he'll be facing. On several occasions, Tiger has traveled to Europe the week before the British Open to get used to links style golf and its intricacies, and to get appropriately rested and psyched to play his best in the event.

Mickelson likes to come early, too, but he preps differently by competing in the Scottish Open on the European Tour—an event he almost won in 2007 (Mickelson lost in a playoff to Gregory Havret).

Take a page out of Phil's and Tiger's book and prepare to peak for your majors. If possible, play the tournament venue a few weeks in advance to get a feel for the layout, length, speed of the greens, etc. Take notes, measure important yardages and get a mental picture of how you'll need to practice and game plan to play your best when it matters most. Do everything that you can to be prepared and you'll be much more confident standing on the first tee come your major.

EVENT SCHEDULING

While your parents and coaches want to be involved in various aspects of your game, it's important that you learn how to plan and manage your own playing schedule, from choosing tournaments to registering for events to budgeting your time and expenses. Taking this sort of initiative helps build responsibility.

As a high-performance athlete, you need to plan your schedule thoroughly, not only for competitive events, but also for practice, coaching, skill development and all other activities—including your academic studies, family and personal interests. This planning is your responsibility and should be in line with the goals you set for yourself. Before endeavoring to fill in your personal calendar and your tournament schedule, take some time to work with your coach to plan your schedule strategy and budget.

TOURNAMENT SCHEDULE PLANNING

Playing too few or too many events is likely to be detrimental to your performance. Competitive golfers need to plan a schedule that gives them an optimal amount of stress and arousal. I'm talking about good stress, the kind that challenges your limits and expands your horizons. There is a difference between being tournament tough, i.e., feeling comfortable with the pressure of competitive golf—and being burned out. Burnout happens when you play so much that every round seems bland and uninspiring. According to research from Dr. John Marshall at the Self Management Group, players need to find the optimal performance zone for their own situation.

SCHEDULING DO'S AND DON'TS

1. Too few events

EVENT SCHEDULING
List the competitive events (in chronological order)
in which you plan to play in the upcoming competitive season.

Date	Title of Event	Location

TOURNAMENT SCHEDULE PLANNING

List the competitive events (in chronological order) in which you plan to play in the upcoming competitive season.

Date	Title of Event	Location

Courtesy of Self Management Group

- Insufficient "good" stress
- Expect less than optimal performance

2. Ideal practice/competitive event ratio
   - Competitor is prepared and rested for competition
   - Has opportunity to build skill
   - Is mentally prepared for optimum performance
3. Too many events
   - Too much stress
   - Skill decay
   - Burnout
   - Can expect less than optimal performance
   - Irritable and lackadaisical

There are several considerations that go into creating a schedule. Your budget will determine how many events you can enter, as will your academic schedule and other obligations. Your age is another consideration: The older you are, the more competitive events you're likely to schedule. Here are some rough guidelines for the number of events you should enter, based on your age:

- Boys ages 9-12, girls ages 8-11 = 5-10 competitions per year
- Boys ages 12-16, girls ages 11-15 = 10-20 competitions per year
- Boys ages 16-18, girls ages 15-17 = 15-25 competitions per year
- Men ages 18-23+, women ages 17-23+ = 15-30 competitions per year

Playing too few events creates insufficient stress and less-than-optimal performance. Playing too many events creates

SCHEDULE PLANNING EXERCISE

For each event you've listed, ask yourself the following questions:

- *Does your schedule allow you to meet your goals?*
- *Do you have room in your schedule for adequate rest, practice, skill development, coaching and personal interests?*
- *Does your schedule allow you to adequately prepare and perform your best in your "majors"?*

too much stress, causing burnout, fatigue, a decline in skills and performance, and increased irritability. With an ideal practice/competition ratio, you'll feel prepared, rested and psyched for competition, and you'll still have the opportunity to build your skills in practice.

SCHEDULING PITFALLS

In golf you're responsible for planning your own competitive schedule, a fairly unique experience in sports. Your competitive schedule needs to fit your age, stage of development and future goals. It's very easy to schedule poorly, which can have a negative impact on your performance and future development. Here are some of the most common scheduling mistakes to watch for—and avoid:

Playing vs. unsuitable competition: As a junior golfer, you need to compete in events that are stimulating and appropriately challenging. Competitive golfers develop best when they gain experience and build confidence

PLANNING SCHEDULE FOR THE MONTH OF _____

Sunday	Monday	Tuesday	Wednesday	Thursday	Friday	Saturday

Notes: _____

(by making birdies and posting good scores) against their contemporaries. There's no need to "skip grades" and compete against adults. This often leads to a loss of confidence, and it can lead to a negative spiral. Michelle Wie and Ty Tryon are well-known examples of this phenomenon, opting to skip AJGA and other junior events in order to compete on the PGA and LPGA Tours as teenagers. If you're at a national/international level for your age, you should compete against like-skilled players whenever possible. Besides, you'll enjoy the camaraderie and social aspect of interacting with others your age more.

Overscheduling: The competitive season can be hectic and taxing both physically and psychologically. Players can compete in events every week if they so choose, but doing so often causes them to fall far short of their potential. They expect that this pattern will lead them to college golf and beyond. This is a dangerous line of thinking. Instead, take a page out of Tiger Woods' book and plan a balanced competitive schedule that is exciting and played on courses that you like. During his best years, Woods would schedule no more than 15 to 20 tournaments, nearly half of them major championships or World Golf Championship events. The rest were made up of courses he experienced great success on like Bay Hill (Arnold Palmer's event), Muirfield Village (the Memorial), Torrey Pines and Cog Hill. The schedule should allow you to arrive at every competition prepared to succeed, and most important, it should ensure that you have enough rest so that you have the best opportunity to peak at the big events—State Junior, U.S. Junior Amateur, State Am, U.S. Am.

Not scheduling adequate time for training, preparation or coaching: You have to put in the effort and energy necessary for daily skill practice (repetition) and coaching. The common mistake young players make is to compete in an event and practice little, if at all, after their rounds. This is not consistent with the principles of elite athlete development—rigorous daily practice in addition to competing is required. During her playing career, LPGA Hall of Famer Annika Sorenstam would be found on the practice range after every competitive round even if she shot a 65. It was part of her regimen, not something she did only after poor rounds or when she needed to work out a few kinks in her swing.

Not planning for rest or personal time: When planning your competitive schedule, mini-breaks should be included. It's recommended you take off one day per week and a long weekend at some juncture during the summer months. It's not advisable to schedule more than three events per month, otherwise you risk getting fatigued or burned out.

Playing with super-high expectations or outcome thoughts: It's unwise to head into a tournament thinking, "I need to get a top 10 in this event." But it's common for young players to feel stressed about posting results that will gain the attention of college coaches. As a result, many players forget what contributes to a good result in the first place—staying in the present, focusing on each shot, and not looking ahead or behind. Build skill with your training and then learn to relax and play your game in competition. Remember how seldom you make a birdie when you try to; just control what you can and play the game.

As you finish your plan, make sure you have the tournament date and registration deadlines noted. Take full responsibility for entering competitions by the due date. When you're finished, you should have a full tournament schedule for your season. Use a calendar so you can get a feeling for the number of weeks or days between events, the start and end date of each training phase and any other events which could play a part in your training.

Budget Planning

It's critical that your goals mesh with your financial resources. Quite frankly, you'll need money in order to achieve your goals. The following worksheet should help you plan a financial strategy commensurate with your performance plan and objectives. To come up with a total budget of needed funds for the year, you need to look at tourney fees, equipment, coaching, travel and other expenses such as food, clothing, transportation, etc. As a junior golfer, you may not have to worry so much about, for example, your car payments, but understanding all the costs involved will help you plan better as you head on to college and perhaps even into a professional career.

Additionally, making a financial plan is part of the overall responsibility of your training and development. Even if your parents help with the costs, it's important you go through the planning process and sit down and discuss the year with them. Making a plan during your pre-season and tracking it through the rest of the year helps you know where you made accurate predictions.

SELF-MANAGEMENT: TAKING FULL RESPONSIBILITY FOR YOUR DEVELOPMENT AND PERFORMANCE

"Self-management is the #1 competency in all top performers." —Dr. John Marshall

THE PRINCIPLES OF SELF-MANAGEMENT

Understand and follow the nine principles of self-management outlined below:

1. *Performance: The Key to Success*

You're accountable for your results, but you are responsible for your performance. Self-managers understand the difference between the two, which are often used interchangeably. Don't make this mistake. Your results are your scores, but you don't have direct control of your results. By this, I mean you can't control what your competition shoots, or what the weather is going to be. Nor can you control your luck. For example, you might play in the morning in pouring rain, while the afternoon competitors enjoy sunny skies and soft fairways and greens. You can complain all you want, but it just as easily could have been you playing in those benign conditions. You can only do the best you can with the conditions you're given.

Self-managers take full responsibility for their performance, all of the effort, focus and attention that goes into giving yourself the best possibility of getting the best results in competition. For example, you're responsible for your pre-event training and preparation, attitude, emotional control, nutrition, hydration, equipment, game plan, self-talk, warm-up, etc.

2. *Expectations Dictate Performance*

If you think you can or you think you can't, you're right. Self-managers have the faith and belief that they can reach the goals they set for themselves. Winners see themselves holding the trophy before the competition begins.

3. *Reinforcement Creates Habits*

Self-managers discover what motivates them. They don't rely on external rewards like trophies or prizes; instead, they're internally driven to enjoy the process involved in improvement and achievement. They play and practice for the love of the game and the challenge of exploring their performance limits.

4. *Motivate Yourself*

Self-managers have the internal drive and passion to set their goals and go for it. They don't need to rely on others to motivate them; however, every once in a while they may need a little push (that 10 percent) from a coach, parent or friend to stay on track.

5. *Maximize Your Return on Energy*

There are three steps to getting the most from your investment of time and energy: (1) Establish what skills need to be improved; (2) set priorities and decide exactly how much time you need to spend on improving the identified skills; and (3) consult with your coach to come up with a plan and put it into action. In competitive golf, a player generally gets the maximum return when he or she follows these three steps, and puts extra practice time in on "The Big 3"—driving, putting and wedge-play skills (which include chipping, pitching and sand play).

6. *Manage Your Effort*

There is only one way to get from objectives to results—effort! I train my athletes to understand that there's only one place where success comes before work—in the dictionary! High achievers put phenomenal amounts of focused energy into improving skill and confidence so that they can perform their best under pressure. Don't look for shortcuts.

7. *Manage Your Self-Confidence*

Expectations can influence your performance, but self-confidence determines your expectations. Recognize your good performances and express satisfaction in them. Think about your achievements to reinforce them. Devote energy to reliving or rehearsing positive events, as well as others' positive reactions and praise.

8. *Commit Yourself*

Change "I should" to "I will." Vow never to use the phrase "I should" again; instead, decide what to do and then set a timetable to do it. If your goal is to improve so that you can hit 10 more greens in regulation per tournament by the time your biggest event of the season rolls around, then do what it takes to making this happen. Self-managers accomplish what they set out to do. Put your energy into these actions, not into thinking about what you should or could do.

9. *Make a Plan and Commit to It*

Plan your work and then work your plan. Establish an action plan and then roll up your sleeves and go to work. Be disciplined to follow your plan even when you might not feel like it—make all of the necessary sacrifices.

BUDGET PLAN

1. Tournament Entry Fees: $ _____
   Determine each entry fee for the tournaments you'll
   be playing and enter the total.

2. Membership Dues: $ _____
   Enter the cost of your golf facility membership or
   school team fees.

3. Green Fees: $ _____
   Enter the amount you plan to spend on miscellaneous
   green fees outside of your facility (practice rounds,
   course practice, etc.).

4. Practice Range Fees: $ _____
   Enter the amount you'll spend on range balls or
   practice facility membership.

5. Practice Range Balls: $ _____
   Enter the amount you plan to spend on practice balls
   at competition sites.

6. FEES SUB-TOTAL: Add 1 to 5 = $ _____

Equipment for the Year

7. Shoes: $ _____
   Estimate your shoe expenses (new shoes, replacement
   spikes, cleaning, etc.) and enter the amount.

8. Gloves: $ _____
   Estimate how much you'll spend on new gloves and
   enter the amount.

9. Balls: $ _____

    Estimate how much you'll spend on balls and enter
    the total.

10. Drivers and Fairway Metals: $ _____

    Determine how much you'll spend on drivers and
    fairway metals and enter the total.

11. Irons: $ _____

    Determine how much you're likely to spend on irons
    and enter the total.

12. Putters: $ _____

    Estimate how much you'll spend on putters and enter
    the total.

13. Wedges: $ _____

    Determine how much you'll spend on wedges and
    enter the total.

14. Bags: $ _____

    Estimate how much you'll spend on bags and enter
    the total. (Don't forget to budget travel bags if you
    have a tournament you'll fly to.)

15. Miscellaneous: $ _____

    Determine how much you'll need to spend on
    incidentals such as re-gripping, re-shafting, and
    training aids and enter the total..

16. SUB-TOTAL: Add 7 to 15 = $ _____

Coaching and Travel

17. Coaching: $ _____

Estimate your total coaching expenses and enter.

18. Accommodations: $ _____

Estimate the cost of hotels and accommodations and enter the total.

19. Gas: $ _____

Estimate how much you'll spend on gas and enter the total.

20. Airline Tickets: $ _____

Determine how much you'll spend on airline tickets as well as extra baggage charges for clubs and gear and enter the total.

21. Food: $ _____

Determine how much you'll spend on food at events as well as on the road and enter the total.

22. SUB-TOTAL: Add 17 to 21 = $ _____

Miscellaneous

23. Food: $ _____

Estimate your food expenses at your home club or snack bar before, during or after practice and enter the total. (Don't forget to budget for energy bars and drinks you buy and carry for practice and play.)

24. Clothing: $ _____

Estimate your total clothing costs and enter the total.

(Don't forget jackets, fleece pullovers, and any team gear, including hats, shirts or jackets that must be purchased.)

25. Vehicle Maintenance: $ _____
    Estimate how much you'll spend on the maintenance of your vehicle and enter the total.

26. Car Payments: $ _____
    Determine how much you'll spend on car payments and enter the total.

27. Car Insurance: $ _____
    Determine how much you'll spend on car insurance this year and enter the total.

28. Miscellaneous: $ _____
    Add up all other anticipated expenses not outlined above and enter the total..

29. SUB-TOTAL: Add 23 to 28 = $ _____

TOTAL EXPENSES
Enter all sub-totals here.
Fees sub-total, number 6: $ _____
Equipment sub-total, number 16 $ _____
Coaching/travel sub-total, number 22 $ _____
Miscellaneous sub-total, number 29 $ _____

TOTAL EXPENSES OVER NEXT 12 MONTHS:
$ _____

6

Effective Practice Strategies: Practicing Technique and The Mental Game

> *"Whether it is playing golf or rugby, litigating, being a chef or playing the piano, the top performers in the world—the champions—not only work harder than everyone in their field but they have invested many more hours of highly focused practice over the years."*
>
> —James Citrin

If you're an aspiring competitive golfer, it's critical you understand the correlation between effective practice habits and improved performance. In this chapter, you'll learn why effective practice gets results, and how to tailor your practice to achieve your goals.

Many talented players lose sight of why they practice in the first place, and their development stagnates. They simply forget the object of the game, which is to put the ball in the hole in the fewest strokes possible. The purpose of your practice is to develop skills that will enable you to shoot lower scores in competition—period! Armed with the knowledge in this chapter, you and your coach will be able to customize

DELIBERATE PRACTICE

Deliberate practice is defined as being engaged in activities specifically designed to improve performance with full concentration.

your practice and training to reach that goal, and to make the process as fun and exciting as possible.

THE SODA MACHINE

In my role as head coach of the Canadian National Men's Team, I've observed hundreds of talented young players with aspirations of playing at the highest level of competitive golf. There's no question that what separates these players in the end is not their inherent talent, but their commitment to training. Research shows that it takes about 10 years and more than 10,000 hours of deliberate practice to ascend to world-class levels of performance in any field. On average, experts engage in deliberate practice for approximately four to five hours per day. It takes time to develop the sustained concentration necessary for deliberate practice, a style of practice much different than that used by many aspiring high-performance golfers.

If you look at the Official World Golf Ranking and the leading money-winners on the PGA and European tours, the players who consistently work the hardest with the most professional habits are the ones who ascend to the top. They do not arrive by chance or accident; they've earned it and they need to continue to earn it, otherwise they'll be replaced by someone else. You have to be willing to pay the price, in time and focus, to ascend to the elite level.

To help my students assess whether their practice habits

are substantial enough, I use the "Soda Machine" metaphor. Imagine you want to buy a soda and it costs $1. If you haven't earned enough quarters, you will not get the soda no matter how hard or how many times you press the button on the machine. It's the same with good results in competition: In order to get rewarded, you need to have earned enough "quarters" from your training.

I always ask my students to self-evaluate their practice habits: How many quarters do they have in their pocket? How hard have they worked and how much improvement have they made in the skills they've identified in their practice plan? When they feel like they have four or more quarters, they're confident of achieving good results. The players who perform the best usually tell me that they have six or more quarters in their pockets when they arrive on the first tee of a competition. This gives them both confidence and competence to perform under pressure—two huge keys for success.

WHAT EFFECTIVE PRACTICE LOOKS LIKE

Most aspiring competitive golfers have never seen effective practice in action or had the opportunity to learn how to practice this way. It's crucial that you're 100 percent clear on this in order to develop into the best golfer you can be. Effective practice is different for everyone. Your practice should suit your own personality, schedule, facility access, and coaching support. However, there are some common pieces that should be in everyone's puzzle, including:

- *Sufficient time*: In order to develop the skills necessary to become a world-class player, you need to practice for three to five hours per day (including on-course practice) for 10 years or longer.

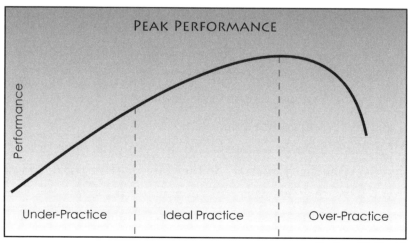

Courtesy of GolfPsych®

Under Practice

Too few hours/insufficient coaching
Practice doesn't fit personality
Uncertain expectations
Low performance confidence
Fear, anxiety
Poor touch, little feel
Bad timing
Poor practice goals
Too social in practice
Feels undeserving of good play
Practice has little purpose or structure
Golf effort does not match game

Ideal Practice

Good quality and quantity
Practice matches personality
Practice has a purpose and matches performance goals
Appropriate coaching and feedback
Balance between mechanics and feel

Great touch, tempo, timing and feel
Great performance confidence
Physical and mental skills remain high
Rested for competition
Minimal injury
Keeps life in balance with golf

Over Practice
Too many hours/too reliant on coach
Practice doesn't fit personality
High expectations
Excessive outcome thinking
Fatigue, burnout
Impatient, easily frustrated
Very mechanical
Overuse injuries and illnesses
Excessively structured practice
Practice for faulty reasons
Little creative practice
Life out of balance with golf

- *A primary focus on the "Big 3"*: By "Big 3" I mean the driver, putter and wedges. All of the shots in golf are important; however, world-class golfers have mastered these clubs.
- *A mixture of training*: You need to include blocked practice, random practice, transfer training, mental-game training, and strength and fitness training in your routine. (Don't worry, if you haven't heard of some of these methods, they're explained later. See "Types of Practice" page 108.)

- *Quality feedback*: It's been said that feedback is the breakfast of champions. Developing golfers need high-quality feedback from several sources, including coaches, video, training aids, launch monitors and GPS rangefinders. Another source of feedback is you and what you see when you hit a shot (the flight of the ball, the size and shape of your divots, etc.).

TYPES OF PRACTICE

Whether it's playing the piano, shooting free throws or hitting golf shots, there's no question that the frequency, quality and intensity of practice plays a huge role in building the skills and confidence necessary to perform successfully under pressure. The following three types of practice are the most effective in terms of getting you prepared to play your best in competition. Below you'll learn how they're different from one another, and how you can use each to your best advantage.

Blocked practice: Blocked practice can be defined as hitting the same shot with the same club to the same target over and over again. It's also commonly referred to as "scraping and hitting." I tell my players to think of blocked practice as hitting a big ice block of balls, with each ball serving as an ice cube. Blocked practice is all about high volume repetition. An example of blocked practice would be hitting drivers on the practice range for 45 minutes to the same target in the distance. It's an effective means for building skills and establishing motor patterns, and can be a major component of your practice; however, it should not be the only way you practice. When practicing in this fashion, establish a precise target and place clubs on the ground to ensure that your alignment is sound (i.e., square to your target) because this type of practice is likely to engrain the pattern that you're repeating.

Random practice: Random practice is different from blocked practice in that there's not such a high volume of repetition. In random practice, a player changes clubs and switches targets frequently. The lie of the ball and the intended curve and trajectory of the shot may be altered as well. The "54-Shot Challenge" developed by former Swedish National Team Coach Pia Nilsson and psychologist Kjell Enhager is a perfect example of random practice. The Swedes believe that it's possible to shoot a perfect round of golf—18 consecutive birdies for a score of 54—in competition. The 54-Shot Challenge is designed to build the skills and confidence necessary to shoot this incredible score. To perform the challenge, you take 54 shots, randomly changing clubs and targets after each shot. Many of these shots are unique, from hitting a driver off your knees to hitting big, intentional hooks and slices, etc. The challenge is one of the keys to the Swedish National Team's success: Players like former LPGA great Annika Sorenstam and 2009 Players champion Henrik Stenson use it regularly in their practice regimens. (Research shows that athletes who train using random practice techniques are likely to outperform those who employ only traditional blocked practice over time.)

Transfer training: Transfer training is simulated practice. It's like a pilot using a flight simulator to learn how to fly—he's training for the real thing and building

54-SHOT CHALLENGE

Evaluate your shots on a scale 1-5, where 5 is exactly what you intended to do. Enter the ranking number in each related box. Hit each shot to a target.

Hit 5 shots to 5 different targets (each shot should use a different club)

1	2	3	4	5

Hit each of these clubs according to the directions in the left column. (Change targets for every shot.)

	7 Iron	5 Iron	3 Iron	3 Wood	Driver
High					
Low					
Hook					
Slice					
Draw					
Fade					

Hit an 8 Iron and watch for where it lands.
Then use these six clubs and carry the ball to the same place.

7 Iron	6 Iron	5 Iron	4 Iron	3 Wood

Hit 3 drives from a kneeling position.

1	2	3

Turn a club around and hit 5 shots from your opposite side, to a target.

1	2	3	4	5

Finish up by hitting 4 shots with 4 different clubs to 4 different targets.

1	2	3	4

Date: _____ Add up the numbers to find **MY SCORE TODAY**: _____

Designed and used by the Swedish National Team

confidence by making the training as realistic as possible. Dr. Christina, an expert in the field of training and practice, encourages players and coaches to use transfer training techniques. One way to put transfer training into action is to simply act on the practice range as you would if you were playing in competition. Imagine the hole that you want to play, analyze the conditions (i.e., examine the wind and lie), select a club and a target, follow your routine, hit the shot and imagine where it would finish on an actual course. On the next shot, predict where you would be on the course, imagine the shot required and hit it as though you were there. Transfer training teaches players to analyze and correct their own performance, as well as develop key visualization and mental-game skills. It enables you to have a seamless transition from the practice tee or green to the course.

PERFORMANCE GOALS

Performance goals are objective measurements and a crucial part of your practice. For example, a scratch player may have a performance goal of hitting 8 of 14 tee shots within a 30-yard-wide area on the range (to mimic a fairway). In the business world, it's commonly said, "That which can be measured can be improved." Setting performance goals in your golf practice will only enhance your confidence and performance in competitive play. It focuses your energy and attention during practice, and can motivate and inspire you to improve. It also makes practice more fun and challenging.

Effective use of transfer training will require less frequent feedback, instruction and coaching. Players should practice their pre-shot routines and mental routines between each shot and putt. They should hit balls with different clubs, and also hit to different distances with the same club. The resulting effect is that shots are more difficult to perform on the practice range than they are during traditional training. Transfer training also tends to promote a more realistic level of confidence.

TIPS FOR MAXIMIZING PRACTICE

It's helpful to keep a written practice journal, so that you can write down practice tips as you discover them. In the meantime, here are a few to get you started:

1. Resist the desire to "rake and hit." Practice with a goal in mind and structure your practice accordingly, even if it's just to establish good tempo and feel. Once you've accomplished that, leave. Practice too long and you risk suffering from fatigue, tension and poor concentration.

2. Adopt your own style of practice not that of others. Always find a balance between drills and play that fits your learning style and current needs. If you're working on learning a new skill, then incorporate more technique into your practice. Do not copy the practice style of someone with a different personality.

3. Practice for the right reasons. You practice to learn and maintain skills not as punishment for poor play, to relieve guilt or boredom, to please someone else, to quell fears of losing ground to others or because you do not know what else to do.

4. Identify and define strategies for strengthening weaknesses. Use a journal to document these strategies and incorporate them into your practice schedule.

5. Maintain a balance between practice and the other important things in your life, such as family, friends, hobbies and other responsibilities. Golf should remain something you do not who you are.

6. Resist practicing too much. Watch for signs of over practice such as outcome thinking, fatigue, burnout, muscle strains and other injuries. If you notice any of these symptoms, take a break and change your approach.

7. Resist under practicing, or not enough. Watch for signs of under practice such as low performance confidence, poor touch, bad timing and tempo, and feeling undeserving of playing well.

8. Practice like you play. Spend at least some of your practice hitting shots just as you would in competition. Use your imagination to simulate competitive situations you may encounter on the course, such as nursing a one-stroke lead with one hole to play. Practice your breathing and mental routine to consistently execute the shots or putts you need to make under the imagined pressure.

9. Play like you practice. Think of how you managed yourself before some of your all-time lowest rounds. If you were relaxed and carefree during your pre-round warm-up, and you chit-chatted or daydreamed between shots, try to emulate these types of things when you play. Challenge yourself to hit shots and putts in competition with the same

composure, peace of mind and tempo you had in one of your very best practice sessions.

10. Always rehearse your pre-shot mental routine on the range prior to play. Take a few moments before several shots to run through the three steps of your mental routine (commit, visualize, feel).

11. Include some creative, imaginative activity during every practice session to stimulate the right side of your brain. Creative practice keeps the athlete in your game instead of just the thinker. It includes such things as warming up your mental routine (along with the physical routine), hitting shots around or through imagined obstacles (such as a tree or goal posts), simulating holes (on the range) you'll play in tournament situations, and playing competitive practice games with yourself or another player, such as creating the shot someone else calls out just as you begin your backswing.

12. Separate mental practice (routine, process, tempo, visualization, great feel, etc.) from physical thinker practice (drills, chalk lines, setup, technique, positions, problem solving, etc.). Doing them both simultaneously will only frustrate you and hurt your game. Before you start, decide which one you're working on and organize your practice accordingly.

WHY TRADITIONAL TRAINING DOESN'T WORK

At the 2002 World Scientific Congress of Golf in St. Andrews, Scotland, Dr. Bob Christina from the University of North Carolina at Greensboro presented a research paper titled, "Why Does Traditional Training Fail to Optimize Playing Performance?" In his paper, traditional golf training was often characterized as simply hitting balls, "scraping and hitting" with little purpose and pressure and without a pre-shot routine. Among the problems with traditional training, or "ball beating," are:

- It's not deliberate practice.
- Players are generally not mentally engaged.
- Players are not encouraged to learn to perform golf skills in context of how shots are actually played on the golf course.
- Players depend too heavily on their coaches.
- There is too little practice of the pre-shot routine.
- Golf skills are taught and practiced under conditions very different than those during play.
- Their practice doesn't simulate the competitive pressures involved in play.
- A player hits balls repeatedly the same distance with the same club.
- A player strokes putts repeatedly from the same distance.
- All shots are struck from good lies.
- Ball beating makes it relatively easy to perform on the practice range.
- It promotes a false sense of confidence.
- There is little focus on reacting to targets.

Traditional training can lull players into feeling they've learned skills which have to be performed during play. However, it can be a strong component if a player combines this with effective random practice and transfer training.

How to Get the Most From Practice
Your practice should be fun but effective; it should reflect

SAMPLE PRACTICE PLAN
Competitive Week for Monday

Time	Schedule
7:00 a.m.	wake up
7:30 a.m.	breakfast in the hotel
8:00 a.m.	
8:30 a.m.	stretch and warm up
9:00 a.m.	pre-game warm up (physical, mental, short game)
9:45 a.m.	tee off (round 1)
10:00 a.m.	
11:00 a.m.	
12:00 p.m.	eating on course (healthy snacks, sandwiches, fruit, lots of water)
1:00 p.m.	
2:00 p.m.	
2:30 p.m.	back to htoel for rest and relaxation
3:00 p.m.	
4:00 p.m.	
4:30 p.m.	practice short game, long game, and putting
5:00 p.m.	
6:00 p.m.	
6:30 p.m.	dinner
7:00 p.m.	
7:30 p.m.	
8:00 p.m.	free time
11:00 p.m.	lights out

YOUR PRACTICE PLAN
Competitive Week for _____

Time	Schedule
7:00 a.m.	
8:00 a.m.	
9:00 a.m.	
10:00 a.m.	
11:00 a.m.	
12:00 p.m.	
1:00 p.m.	
2:00 p.m.	
3:00 p.m.	
4:00 p.m.	
5:00 p.m.	
6:00 p.m.	
7:00 p.m.	
8:00 p.m.	

SAMPLE PRACTICE PLAN
Non-Competitive Week for Wednesday

Time	Schedule
7:00 a.m.	
8:00 a.m.	wake up
8:30 a.m.	shower and change
9:00 a.m.	breakfast
9:30 a.m	arrive at golf course
9:30 a.m. to 10:15 a.m.	putting practice and drills
10:15 a.m. to 11:15 a.m.	chipping, pitching, and lob shot practice
11:15. a.m. to noon	lunch break
noon to 1:30 p.m.	full swing practice and training: 45 mins. blocked practice; 45 mins. "54 Shot Challenge"
1:30 p.m. to 1:45 p.m.	break
1:45 p.m. to 2:00 p.m.	pre-round warm-up: putting and chipping
2:00 p.m. to 4:15 p.m.	play 9 holes
4:15 p.m. to 4:30 p.m.	break
4:30 p.m. to 5:15 p.m	full swing practice, random practice, change target/clubs
5:30 p.m.	dinner
6:15 p.m.	personal/social time
11:00 p.m.	lights out

YOUR PRACTICE PLAN
Non-Competitive Week for _____

Time	Schedule
7:00 a.m.	
8:00 a.m.	
9:00 a.m.	
10:00 a.m.	
11:00 a.m.	
12:00 p.m.	
1:00 p.m.	
2:00 p.m.	
3:00 p.m.	
4:00 p.m.	
5:00 p.m.	
6:00 p.m.	
7:00 p.m.	
8:00 p.m.	

your personality. Looking for some tips on how to maximize the quality of your practice sessions and keep them fresh? Try some of these ideas:

- Arrive at your practice session with a specific plan and performance goal.
- Play fun on-course practice games such as "worst-ball scramble" (i.e., playing from the worst tee shot in your group), or "Par 18," a nine hole "up-and-down" game where all holes are scored as par 2s. (You create your own holes with different lies and turf conditions, or by randomly changing shots and targets.)
- Train on the course whenever possible. There's no better place to practice and simulate tournament conditions than actually being on the course.
- Measure your performance and create pressure as much as possible. For example, commit yourself to practicing lob shots over a bunker until you hole three shots, or practice rolling different-length putts with a friend for a friendly wager.
- Don't forget to focus your energy on your strengths. Build them to an even higher level.
- Identify opportunities for improvement (i.e., your weakest links). Be committed to improving each of these skills over time until they become strengths under pressure.
- Practice your short game twice as much as your long game. Use the "Red Zone Short Game Skills Test" for motivation (see page 152).
- Make your training as realistic and as simulated to golf as possible.

- Keep a written journal of your practice activities; share this with your coach.

PRACTICE MISTAKES TO AVOID

When quizzed about their reasons for practicing, many struggling players reveal faulty motivations, such as guilt, anxiety, boredom and frustration. Have you ever practiced for one or more of these reasons? If so, check out the accompanying suggestions, courtesy of Dr. Deborah Graham and John Stabler of GolfPsych.

Guilt: You feel that if you don't put in a specific number of practice hours per week, you're unworthy of playing good golf. It may even have occurred to you that if you don't work hard enough, you're not a worthy person in any regard.

Suggestion: Take steps to understand how you've come to tie your identity so closely to your golf. Strengthen your self-esteem.

Anxiety: You're tormented by the thought that for every hour you don't practice, someone is gaining ground on you competitively. You feel unable to relax unless you put in some practice time.

Suggestion: Shift your emphasis from others to you. Learn to feel at peace before and during (and even without) your practice. Progress is entirely individual and related more to "how" you're practicing rather than "how much."

Release of frustration: Banging balls on the range helps you to get out your frustrations, whether they are related to your golf or something else in your life you're upset about.

Suggestion: While beating balls might provide a release, it seldom improves your game or helps you resolve the underlying problem. Take steps to talk with someone about the problem(s) to resolve them, rather than just trying to alleviate the symptoms. Keep your practice a more productive and positive experience.

Boredom: You often find yourself hitting balls because you're expected to, often with no goal and little purpose.

Suggestion: Set meaningful goals to practice with a purpose, or find something else to do with your time. Practicing with little focus or purpose seldom helps your game and can actually make it worse.

Escape: Life often gets to be too much for you, and the best relief is to lose yourself in your golf.

Suggestion: In addition to finding relief from life's challenges, look for ways to proactively manage them so that they don't end up managing you. Your golf will ultimately be better for it.

Social connection: Golf gives you the chance to be social and meet other people.

Suggestion: If golf is your social outlet, you need to take a look at how you organize your practice. Plan your practice so you have quality time to work on your skills, balanced with intermittent social breaks to keep it fun and interesting for you.

To make someone else happy: You practice because certain other people tell you to and you want to make them happy.

Suggestion: To get the most out of your practice and your golf, you must have a passion for the game. At some point, you must decide to play and practice primarily for yourself. This is especially true of juniors who take up the game to please a parent or someone else they care about.

Under-emphasizing weaknesses: When you practice, you prefer hitting those shots you execute the best because you want to leave feeling good about your game.

Suggestion: You can begin and end your practice by playing to your strengths, but somewhere in-between you need to spend time improving your weaknesses. This is how you develop an all-around game and the confidence necessary to play your best week in and week out.

Over-emphasizing mechanics: So much of your practice time is dedicated to drills, fundamentals and the mechanics of the swing that when you compete, you find yourself obsessed with doing things like correcting your swing and checking certain positions. You're unable to play athletically, which means being able to visualize shots and maintain good feel and tempo.

Suggestion: Set aside some of your time for "right brain practice" or, in other words, to practice as you play. Invent games, be creative with your shotmaking, hit to various targets and, most importantly, practice your pre-shot routine. If you need guidance in any of these areas, a qualified golf coach or sports psychologist can help you with these and other challenges.

UNDER PRACTICING

If you have a hard time picking yourself up off the sofa and getting yourself to practice (with enthusiasm and focus), then chances are you suffer from one or more of the following under-practice symptoms:

Low performance confidence: You haven't been practicing the shots that give you the most trouble. As a result, you don't have the performance confidence to fully commit to these shots in competition.

Poor touch and feel: You don't have your best touch and feel, particularly around the greens; therefore, you struggle to develop any type of consistency with your short game.

Bad timing/tempo: The timing and rhythm of your swing and stroke is not as fluid and athletic as it can be.

Conscious (or subconscious) feelings of being undeserving of good play: You blame yourself for not practicing enough to play well. Taking it one step further, this guilt makes you feel undeserving of playing well.

OVER PRACTICING

If you find that you're always on the practice range or course, then you might exhibit some of the following "workaholic" tendencies, which can be very bad for your game. Check to see if you are experiencing any of them in your own play.

Unchecked expectations/outcome thoughts:
Excessive practice tends to propel you toward higher expectations and performance-inhibiting "outcome thoughts." Your underlying attitude is, "I've put in so many hours, there's no reason I shouldn't post a really low score today." If this is your attitude, you'll be much less tolerant of mistakes and more likely to react emotionally.

Fatigue: Before you realize it, signs of fatigue appear in your game. You find it harder to make decisions and commit to them, to visualize shots and to remain patient with your caddie and those around you. Once you get in an irritable mood, it's hard to repress it.

Burnout: Prolonged fatigue can lead to reduced passion for the game to the point where you start to dislike the game.

Compromised personal life: Over practice reflects a life that is out of balance. While the effects may not be felt immediately, it's likely that long-term neglect of family, marriage, friends and personal/spiritual needs will eventually inhibit your play. This is particularly true if those you care about give up hope that you'll eventually choose to spend more time with them.

PRACTICE DRILLS

Effective practice drills make this all-important time

more enjoyable and competitive. The following drills can be motivating and lead to enhanced skill and confidence:

"20 Putts" Drill: Find a putt on the practice green with some modest break to it. Set up four different lines of coins (or tees) at 3', 4', 5', 6' and 9' from the hole, so that you're putting to the hole from four different directions (East, West, North, South). Putt all of the 3-, 4-, 5-footers and so on. Keep track of your misses. Tournament class players convert 16 of 20 putts. PGA Tour players make 18 of 20.

"4-Footers" Drill: Mark a spot on the putting green with a tee approximately four feet from a hole. (Note: The putt should be as flat and easy as possible.) See how many consecutive 4-foot putts you can make. World-class competitors can make 50 or more consecutive 4-footers; PGA Tour players, 100 plus.

"Birdie Putt" Drill: Measure a spot 20 feet from a hole on the putting green. Place tees or coins in a two-foot inverted semi-circle (i.e., "safe zone") from the front of the hole to behind the hole. Take 10 putts. See how many go in or finish within the safe zone. Aspiring competitors should be able to place at least seven putts inside the safe zone; PGA Tour players should finish 10 for 10.

"Sand Play" Drill: Scatter balls in various lies in a greenside bunker and practice until you hole out three shots. Alternate targets for each shot.

"Chipping" Drill: Scatter balls in various lies around a

practice green and chip until you hole three shots with each club that you're using. (Note: Chipping requires various clubs to produce different amounts of roll and carry.)

Practicing the Mental Game

Many pro golfers will tell you that 80 percent of the game is mental, so it's critical to understand how to practice and improve your mental game. You need to know which skills to acquire, and then how to practice and evaluate them. A sports psychologist or PGA Teaching Professional with sufficient training and background in this area can help you in this process.

If you're limited by time or cost constraints, there are some excellent resources on mental game practice that you can learn on your own, such as Dr. Karl Morris's *Train Your Golf Brain* CD (golf-brain.com), the Subconscious Training Corporation's *Golf Mind and Putting Mind* CDs (directyourmind.com); and an excellent number of books, including *The Inner Game of Golf* by Timothy Gallwey; *Every Shot Must Have a Purpose* by Pia Nilsson and Lynn Marriott; *The 8 Traits of Champion Golfers* by Deborah Graham and Jon Stabler; *Extraordinary Golf* by Fred Shoemaker; *How Great Golfers Think* by Bob Skura; and *The Little Red Book* by Harvey Penick.

The 8 Traits of Champion Golfers

You may wonder how a pro can hit a clutch shot on the 72nd hole to win a title when he or she should be nervous and exhausted. Champion golfers work hard to develop several key strengths in their mental game. Dr. Deborah Graham and Jon Stabler, co-founders of GolfPsych (golfpsych.com), have worked with dozens of top golf professionals to hone their mental-game practice skills. In their book *The 8 Traits of Champion Golfers*, they identify the following characteristics:

1. **Good Focus**
   Good mental routine for each shot. Open focus between shots. Not distracted.

2. **Abstract Thinking**
   Thoughts focus on relevant variables only. Doesn't over-think or over-analyze.

3. **Emotionally Stable**
   Little reaction to poor shots and bad breaks or to good shots and good breaks.

4. **Dominant**
   Moderately aggressive. Takes smart risks. Challenges the course.

5. **Tough-Minded**
   Self-reliant. Indifferent to others. Overcomes adversity. Unaffected by conditions.

6. **Confident**
   Secure, self-satisfied and guilt-free. Sees self as a winner.

7. **Self-Sufficient**
   Very decisive and prefers own decisions. Resists peer pressure.

8. **Optimal Arousal**
   Aware of and controls level of tension to enhance performance. On 1-10 scale: 4 for putting, 6 for driving.

LOOKING FOR MENTAL SOLUTIONS TO PROBLEM SHOTS

It's important that a player combine both the physical and mental aspects of the game while competing. Learn to play golf, don't just focus on making a swing. Follow a pre-shot ritual that enables you to make prudent club choices and strategic decisions then get into position physically with your set-up fundamentals, and imagine the flight of the ball and feel of the swing. Relax and let your swing happen. Most players start analyzing their mechanics as soon as they hit a poor shot, activating their left-brain thinking and making it harder to perform. If they weren't doing it before, they now try to use mechanical swing thoughts which, most of the time, don't work. The vast majority of poor shots for competitive golfers are due to mental errors, which lead to physical ones.

After any shot or putt that doesn't come off well, you should ask yourself the following four questions, which are based on the work and research of Dr. Deborah Graham and Jon Stabler of GolfPsych:

1. How was my tempo or rhythm? If the answer is, "It wasn't good" or "Too quick," then your goal for the next shot or putt is to have really good tempo or rhythm.

2. How was my commitment to my club, target and type of shot? If the answer is, "I wasn't committed to any of them" or "I was changing over the ball," then the goal for the next shot or putt is to be committed to your decisions.

3. How was my visualization? If the answer is, "I didn't visualize the shot" or "I didn't take time in my routine" or "I couldn't see the shot as well as usual," then the goal for the next shot or putt is to visualize it much better.

4. How was my feel? If the answer is, "I didn't feel the shot" or "I skipped the feel step," then the goal for

the next shot is to emphasize the feel step of the routine.

By looking at the mental side for a reason and a solution first, you'll be emphasizing the mental side and utilizing your right-brain abilities. This will help prevent a series of bad shots and bad holes. It will also help you keep your level of arousal and emotions in check.

GolfPsych Mental Performance Chart

The bubble exercise, on the next page, by Dr. Graham is an extremely effective way for you to understand what goes into your ideal performance state (often referred to as "The Zone"). It also helps you recognize when your thoughts and focus have gone outside this zone, or bubble, leading to less than optimal performance. To complete this exercise, consider:

- Think about a round where you performed your best. Now, inside the Champion Circle or bubble, jot down everything you remember about that experience. Often, players write things such as: "Felt relaxed," "Recovered from my bad shots," "Didn't get ahead of myself," etc.
- Think about a round that was important to you where you played poorly. Outside of the Champion Circle, jot down what that experience was like. Players commonly write things such as: "Felt very tense"; "Focused on my swing mechanics"; "Bad attitude"; etc.
- Be aware of what you wrote in your Champion Circle bubble. Do your best to be in this state when you play.

MENTAL PERFORMANCE CHART

Name: _____

Event: _____

Performance Goals: _____

Comments: _____

Date: _____

Results: _____

OUTCOME

AVERAGE

PROCESS

CHAMPION

OUTCOME

AVERAGE

Courtesy of GolfPsych®

- Be aware of what you wrote outside the circle. Do your best not to "go there" when you play. When you do, catch yourself, refocus, and get your thoughts and actions back into the Champion Circle as soon as possible.
- Set a Performance Goal before you play and write it down on the Performance Goals line (i.e., to be in the bubble for 75% of your shots). Keep score of this when you play and record this on the Results line.
- Reflect on your rounds after play to evaluate your mental game, and share this sheet with your coach.
- The more time that you spend in the bubble, the more likely it is that you'll perform your best when it matters.

THE ZONE

Use this information by GolfPsych as a quick method of identifying factors that are interfering with your "Zone." Your moods and attitudes will fluctuate with life experiences and circumstances.

POOR PERFORMANCE
No Focus
No goals, no routine, no desire, no purpose. Focus is wide.

Abstract Thinking Limited
Not considering all variables in shotmaking and course management

Depressed Emotions
Flat, down, sad, etc.

Not Dominant
Very passive, low risk taker

Not Tough-Minded
Sensitive. Concern for others

No Confidence
Very self-blaming, guilt prone, insecure and worrying

No Self-Sufficiency
Basket case, cannot make own decisions

Very Low Arousal
Very low energy, unmotivated, little purpose

AVERAGE PERFORMANCE
Drifting Focus
Poor regulation of focus, poor routine and goals, some desire and purpose

Abstract Thinking
Weak, considers some variables and aspects of each shot

Emotions Moderate
Somewhat down, golf is more work than fun

Dominance Moderate
Takes few risks, often playing it safe

Moderately Tough-Minded
Has some discomfort beating others, some concern for others

Poor Confidence
Hard on self, weak self-image

Moderate Self-Sufficiency
Can make some decisions, but may not be committed

Low Arousal
Some motivation but will give up too easily, too relaxed
to focus

PEAK PERFORMANCE
Good Focus
Good focus and great mental routine, narrow focus for
the shot, widen focus between shots

Abstract Thinking
Abstract thinking on relevant variables only, and on
course management when appropriate

Emotionally Stable
Little reaction to bad shots or bad breaks, limited
reaction to good shots

Dominant
Competitive, moderately aggressive, takes smart risks,
challenges the course

Tough-Minded
Self-reliant, indifferent to others, makes own decisions

Confident
Secure, self-satisfied, guilt-free, sees self as winner

Very Self-Sufficient
Very decisive, committed to shots, makes own decisions

Optimal Arousal
Energetic, motivated to succeed, energy to manage routine, regulate focus, keeps thoughts simple, tempo is good

AVERAGE PERFORMANCE
Shifting Focus
Narrows on wrong subjects, mechanics, trouble, fear

Abstract Thinking
Excessive, over thinking shots, mind is too busy, on many things

Emotions High
Impatient, antsy, on edge, strong reaction to bad shot or bad luck

Too Dominant
Too aggressive, takes too many risks, forcing shots, erratic behavior

Excessively Tough-Minded
Selfish, indifferent to others' feelings

Extreme Confidence
Visions of greatness without dedication to steps to achieve greatness

Too Self-Sufficient
Disregards useful input from competent caddy, teacher, wife, etc.

Overly Aroused

Too stressed, mind busy, body tense, visualization inhibited, tempo faster and swing changes

POOR PERFORMANCE
Skewed Focus
Jumps ahead, behind, to trouble, to noise, etc.

Abstract Thinking
Extreme abstract thinking, mind very busy, in a whirl, too much analysis

Emotions Extreme
Anger, frustration, disappointment, dread

Dominance Extreme
Very aggressive, extreme risks taken, very erratic play

Extremely Tough Minded
Very self-centered, often at the expense of others

False Confidence
Illusions of grandeur, dreams exceed reality, unwilling to pay dues

Extremely Self-Sufficient
Refuses assistance, often blames others for mistakes

Extremely Aroused
Very stressed, frustrated, overwrought, focus is lost, emotions become extreme, tempo is very fast

Mental Pre-Shot Routine Checklist

Competitive golfers need to understand the importance of having a pre-shot routine as well as a physical routine. It needs to be practiced and made a habit. The purpose of a mental pre-shot routine is to prepare yourself to hit a shot toward your intended target, and to cue yourself appropriately so that you have the best chance for success. To peak perform you need to have your body ready and your mind devoid of "technique thoughts." Your focus should be external (on the target, tempo or a simple execution thought) versus internal (focus on your swing technique or how to move your body). The following is a mental pre-shot routine checklist. By implementing a strong pre-shot routine that has strategic, physical and mental components, you can make significant performance gains.

Pre-Shot Routine Checklist

1. First, focus on your strategy and tactics. Make your decisions regarding club selection and shot strategy.

2. Second, then take your set-up and get comfortable.

3. Third, mentally shift your focus to the external. Focus on the target with your eyes and visualize the intended flight of the ball. Focus on swinging in good rhythm and balance. You can have a swing thought or performance cue that is swing related if you like, whatever works for you; however, it should not be too complex or technique oriented. The simpler the better.

4. Finally, relax and trust yourself. Move your focus externally and try your best to hit your target.

WHY HAVE A MENTAL PRE-SHOT ROUTINE?

1. Having you practice and focus on your mental pre-shot routine lessens distractions, reduces self-talk clutter, and aids greatly in narrowing your focus to the target before your swing.
2. It helps you to focus on playing golf, not perfecting your golf swing.
3. It also shifts your focus outward to the target (externally), which is how champions perform.

MORE TIPS FOR A GOOD MENTAL GAME

Formulate a realistic game plan: You should make wise strategic choices by focusing on your strengths and weaknesses and your actual skill level. Competitors need to learn to play in the present (one shot at a time) and strive to shoot their personal par. You will learn to make intelligent shot selections because you will become aware of the odds.

Focus on target attachment before pulling the trigger: Target attachment means being focused on the target and the desired flight of the ball. When a player is attached to his target, his focus is external on the target rather than internal on his swing. It is critical for you to play with a "quiet mind" in order to perform optimally. Your coach can help you by teaching you to shift your focus externally and to "attach yourself to the target" just before you begin to swing. Like all skills, both physical and psychological, these will be learned through focused repetition.

"See" the putts fall in real time: You need to set your conscious mind aside on the putting green. There

should not be any conscious thought of technique once you have committed to the line and speed of the putt. "See" the ball roll on the intended line and "hear" it fall in the hole during practice strokes.

Train your eyes and imagination in the short game: Stare intently at the target for about four seconds. Retain this image as you come back to the ball then hit your shot with the image of the target in the front of your mind.

Complete commitment to the target: It's necessary to differentiate between technique practice and "golf" practice. When practicing and refining technique, the focus may be on the movement or refinement, not on a specific target. Conversely, when practicing how to play and hit shots, there should be an absence of technical thoughts and cues; instead, you must be completely committed to the target and the feel of your swing.

MENTAL GAME QUESTIONNAIRE
Courtesy of GolfPsych

Name: _____

Date: _____

Rate yourself on the following areas of your mental game from 1-10 with 1 as NEVER and 10 as ALWAYS.

Concentration and Focus

1. I have a strong mental pre-shot routine which includes: calculating the best shot, committing

to my choices, visualizing the flight of the ball to my target, and feeling my stroke without using mechanical thoughts to make my swing. _____

2. I use my mental pre-shot routine on every shot and putt. _____

3. I relax enough to visualize my shots and see them very clearly. _____

4. I have a feel-type swing thought I use when putting (like Sam Snead's "oily" or "smooth" roll). _____

5. I'm not distracted by people or noise when playing a shot. _____

6. I can quiet my mind and focus well when the pressure is on. _____

7. During competitive rounds, I focus on playing one shot at a time to the best of my ability. _____

Subtotal ÷ 7 = Average Score _____

Thought and Control

8. I'm able to focus on the shot at hand then take my mind off the round between shots. _____

9. I can use negative thoughts and fears as cues or reminders to refocus my thoughts to things I can control (routine, positive self-talk, etc.). _____

10. Before and during the round, I'm thinking positive thoughts that help me stay calm and conserve mental energy. _____

11. When I miss a shot or experience a poor result, I don't berate myself or react emotionally with anger or frustration. _____

12. In the days leading up to a competition, I effectively manage fears of failing, being embarrassed, disrespected by other players, hitting poor shots, choking, yipping, etc. _____

13. During competition, I avoid becoming distracted by or irritated with my playing partners. _____

14. I don't let bumpy greens, spike marks, deep rough, bad weather, slow play, bad rulings, etc., bother or upset me. _____

15. I allow my previous shot or shots to have no influence on my next shot. _____

16. I allow my score to have little influence on my attitude or strategy. _____

17. When I find my thoughts centering on negatives or causing more emotions, I change those thoughts to ones that calm and help me remain positive. _____

18. I'm very aware of my best competitive attitude and thoughts. I work to maintain them before and during competition. _____

19. I manage problems or situations in other areas of my life so they don't distract me when competing. _____

Subtotal ÷ 12 = Average Score _____

Tension Management

20. I stay alert to my own signs of increasing tension (clenched teeth, drawn shoulders, short and quick breaths, loss of feel, etc.). _____

21. I check my level of tension before and during competition. _____

22. I'm aware of physical changes when my tension increases. _____

23. I know how to lower my tension and practice lowering my tension daily. _____

24. I'm aware of mental changes when my tension increases (busy mind, indecisiveness, difficulty visualizing, etc.). _____

25. I use at least one technique for lowering my tension before and during competition. _____

26. My mental pre-shot routine effectively relaxes me and sharpens my focus. _____

27. Part of my short game pre-shot routine includes techniques for calming and lowering my tension when needed. _____

Subtotal ÷ 8 = Average Score _____

Confidence

28. I like myself regardless of how well I play. _____

29. I anticipate good outcomes. _____

30. When I shoot a higher score than usual, I don't like it but I can usually "shake if off" within an hour. _____

31. When I miss a shot or putt, I don't take it personally or berate myself. _____

32. Between shots, I frequently compliment myself on things I did well, and look forward to the next shot opportunity. _____

33. When my physical game is slumping, I refuse to let it ruin my attitude toward my golf or my life. _____

34. I can think of five things I like about myself quickly and easily. _____

Subtotal ÷ 7 = Average Score _____

Mental Preparation, Imagery and Attitude

35. I set mental goals for each competitive round (definite target, good tempo, etc.) and let physical ones like greens and fairways hit, number of putts, etc., take care of themselves. _____

36. I visualize playing the course, or at least the most difficult holes, in preparation for competition. _____

37. I visualize the conditions as they're likely to play and see myself dealing with those conditions successfully before competition. _____

38. I take time before the round to adopt an attitude that will enhance my play, such as my attitude in previous good performances (patient, peaceful, decisive, positive, etc.). _____

39. I mentally re-play poor shots as I would like to play them before competing on the same course again. _____

40. I've identified and readied myself for challenges, both good (such as high expectations) and bad (such as an annoying playing partner.) _____

41. I commit to my game plan and resist changing it based on how I'm playing or scoring. _____

42. I choose my club, target and type of shot based on the weather forecasted the night before competition. _____

43. My game plan is based on the current strengths of my game, not the course design. _____

44. I resist changing my game plan unless the weather dictates it or it's absolutely necessary, and I'm certain I have the confidence and relaxed state to carry it out. _____

45. I set mental goals for my play (things like patience, good mental routines on 80% of my shots, etc.), not physical ones, and rate them after each round. _____

46. My game plan recognizes my strengths and incorporates strategies that give me the maximum opportunity to hit shots I can effectively execute a majority of the time. _____

Subtotal ÷ 12 = Average Score _____

Your Total Mental Game Score

(Add all average scores ÷ 5) _____

USING YOUR MENTAL GAME SCORES

Area Subtotals

Average Score: 7-10

Consider yourself a champion in this area! Rate yourself periodically and take appropriate steps to keep this area strong.

Average Score: 5-6

You are moderately successful at managing this area of your mental game.

Average Score: 1-4

You are weak in this area. Set goals for strengthening this area. For guidance, talk with your golf coach.

Total Mental Game Score

Average Score: 7 or higher

Congratulations! If you were objective in your ratings, you're thinking like a champion. Continue your ratings and try to keep your total average score above a 7.

Average Score: 5-6

You're close to thinking like a champion, but you need to sharpen a few areas to be your best. Make a list of your weaker ratings and find steps to strengthen them with your coaches.

AVERAGE SCORE: 4 OR LOWER

You're not getting the most out of your physical skills because your mental skills are weak. Choose one area at a time, make a list of your weaknesses in each area and decide on a plan for strengthening them. As your mental game scores improve, so will your play—and your enjoyment of the game!

7

SKILLS ASSESSMENT:
THE FOUNDATION OF THE IMPROVEMENT PROCESS

"Feedback is the breakfast of champions."

—Ken Blanchard

The saying "What is measured can be improved" is one of my core coaching beliefs. If you're serious about reaching your potential, it's crucial to evaluate your skill level in every area of the game, from driving to putting. When you begin to measure your performance objectively, you may be surprised to discover how good you are at some skills compared to other athletes in your target group. This can serve as a source of confidence. You may also be surprised to learn that there are some skills you need to develop more than you originally thought, which can inspire you to work more diligently in the future.

In the fall of 2007, former Masters champion Mike Weir invited several top performing junior golfers to Palm Springs, California to train and play with him. The event spoke volumes about Mike's dedication to the next generation, and was a huge thrill for those players in attendance. For one of the players, a student of mine named Matt Hill, interacting with Mike was

was a life-changing experience. In the course of playing and practicing for a few days with Mike, Matt was surprised to discover that he was nearly the equal of Mike in ball-striking; however, he saw a significant gap with regard to his wedge play, short game and game-management tactics. He realized that if he ever wanted to become a professional golfer, he had to work much harder to improve in these and other areas.

The experience that Matt had with Mike was invaluable. It enabled Matt to objectively compare and contrast his skills with a major champion on the course in a quasi-competitive way. It let Matt know that he wasn't as far away from being a PGA Tour player as he may have thought in terms of ball-striking skills, and it shined a light on his weaknesses (i.e., wedge play, short game and course management). Matt came back from his time with Mike and worked feverishly to improve. His resulting development was incredible—a TrackMan assessment of Matt's skills at a training camp at PGA Village in Port St. Lucie, Florida in January 2009 revealed that his ball control and consistency were well above-average for even a PGA Tour player. While I know Matt was a truly elite young player, I could not have predicted what would happen next—after leaving the camp, he returned to North Carolina State University where he went on to have perhaps the most outstanding season ever by an NCAA Division I male golfer. As a sophomore at N.C. State that spring, Matt bested several of Tiger Woods' collegiate records, winning eight events, including the ACC Conference Championship, NCAA Regionals and NCAA Individual Championship at Inverness CC in Toledo, Ohio. He ran the table with respect to the end-of-season awards: named NCAA Player of the Year, NCAA 1st Team All-America, ACC Player of the Year and ACC Athlete of the Year. It was an accomplishment unheard of for a golf athlete. Tiger invited Matt to play in the AT&T Championship at Congressional CC that June, where Matt made the cut in his first PGA Tour start. He played his practice rounds there with, you guessed it, Mike Weir.

While you may never get to pit your skills against a Tour player firsthand like Matt did, you can still measure your performance against the best and see where you stand. Today, coaches have numerous resources, including software-based tracking programs and performance collection tools, to help you track your progress and compare it to the pros. In this chapter, I'll introduce you to some of the possibilities available to you, which include tests for the short game and a cutting-edge computer putting technique analyzer. I'll also introduce you to ShotByShot.com, the world's leading online skills-tracking system that both Matt and I use to collect and analyze data.

ASSESSING YOUR SKILLS

Skill assessment is a foundational piece in the improvement/development process for aspiring competitive golfers. Just as it's crucial for sprinters and their coaches to know how fast the athlete can run the 100-meter dash, it's imperative for golfers (and their coaches) to know how far they hit their clubs, how accurate they are with their clubs, and how proficient they are at getting the ball close to the hole in the short game. Once a golfer has his skills assessed, then he can be aware of his strengths, improve upon them, and play to them on the course. Skills assessment is also very helpful at identifying your "weaknesses," or those specific skills that need to be improved.

Highly skilled and experienced golf coaches have developed what's referred to in sports science as the "coach's eye"—they use their training and experience to "see" the movement patterns, shot characteristics, and overall performance characteristics of a player. Some coaches still rely on this skill-set to assess athletes because, until recently, there wasn't too much else to go by. But in today's modern high-tech world, many high performance coaches use both their "coach's eye" and empirical testing equipment and tools to evaluate skill and measure improvement. More and more professionals are incorporating game-assessment tools into their coaching, such as the TrackMan radar-based golf swing and ball flight analysis system; ShotByShot.com comparative stats collection program; TOMI computerized putting technique evaluation system; and the Red Zone Short Game Skills Test. In addition, three-dimensional (3D) motion capture systems that measure kinematic sequence efficiency are becoming increasingly more popular.

TrackMan

TrackMan is the most advanced and sophisticated golf-skills testing technology ever invented. The system uses 3D Doppler radar, making it golf's version of an MRI machine. TrackMan measures the exact three-dimensional club movement and ball flight, and provides precise data on the ball's launch, flight and landing. TrackMan measures your clubhead speed, ball speed, spin rate, launch angle, carry and roll-out yardages, trajectory, clubface position and dispersion patterns, among other things. This makes it a phenomenal skills evaluation tool and training system.

TrackMan is used each week on the PGA Tour and other worldwide tours. In fact, more than 50 PGA and European Tour players have purchased their own personal units. All of golf's major equipment manufacturers use it for fitting and testing, and the USGA and R&A use it for research and development (R&D) as well as rules compliance testing.

BALL SPEED OF DRIVER SHOTS

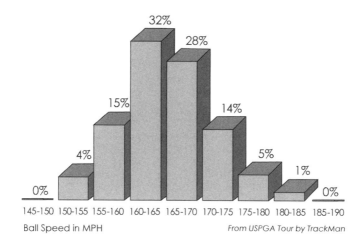

Ball Speed in MPH   *From USPGA Tour by TrackMan*

I've been a TrackMan owner since 2006, and simply can't imagine coaching without it. I use TrackMan to assess a student's ball-striking skills by having him or her hit five solid shots toward specific targets with each club in their bag. This takes about 45 minutes. After the player has finished, we review the results together, often comparing data to PGA/LPGA Tour averages. The results make it clear where the student is strong and where they need to improve.

TrackMan has a gaming feature which enables a golfer to test himself at different yardages. For example, we use the 90-yard wedge game to test a player's primary wedge-play proficiency. The player takes 10 shots to a target at 90 yards. Then TrackMan calculates where all of the balls land in relation to the target and scores the shots. The player is given a relative "handicap" for the skill and can compare his ability to others and to PGA Tour players. I utilize the TrackMan Combine Test to assess the most elite players. This is a 60-shot test that provides very in-depth skills performance data. At the time of printing, Luke Donald, currently No. 1 in the Official World Golf Ranking, has the highest recorded TrackMan Combine Test score to date.

ShotByShot.com

Another useful way to analyze your performance is through an online golf statistics program. I use ShotByShot.com invented by Peter Sanders of Golf Research Associates from Stamford, Connecticut. Golfers record the shots they hit during play on a simple to use scorecard, or they can simply recall them after their round is over if their memory is sufficient. Then they log into the ShotByShot.com website and enter the shots along with relevant course information. ShotByShot.com provides extremely useful information that is much more advanced and sophisticated than traditional statistical programs with a proprietary comparative analysis feature. Golfers and their coaches see in detail a player's relative handicap skill level for all skills, which are then compared to their target handicap group and to PGA Tour players.

Once you enter data for a round, the system makes recommendations on areas for improvement. For example, it may show that you made more than 50 percent of your putts from the 6- to 10-foot range but only 10 percent from 11 to 15 feet. This tells you that you need to spend more time practicing the latter putts. ShotByShot.com allows you to see how many shots could be saved if you were to improve to the level of your target handicap group. As the system analyzes the remaining areas of your game, golfers can see where they need the most improvement.

Red Zone Short Game Skills Test

The Red Zone Short Game Skills Test is an outstanding evaluation tool that I use with my students. This test was created by Top 100 Teacher Charlie King, the Director of Instruction at Reynolds Plantation in Georgia. Charlie modified the testing and evaluation procedure originally designed by PGA Master

Red Zone Short Game Skills Test Evaluation Chart

BUNKER	WEDGE	PITCH	LAG PUTTING	CHIPPING	PUTTING	OVERALL HANDICAP
20 = +5	20 = +5	22 = +5	24 = +5	22 = +5	26 = +5	107+ = +
18 = +3	18 = +3	20 = +3	22 = +3	20 = +3	24 = +3	106 = =
16 = =	16 = =	18 = =	20 = =	18 = =	20 = =	95-99 = 2
15 = 1	15 = 1	17 = 1	18 = 2	17 = 2	18 = 3	90-94 = 3
14 = 2	14 = 3	16 = 2	17 = 4	16 = 4	16 = 6	80-84 = 5
13 = 3	13 = 4	15 = 4	16 = 6	15 = 6	14 = 9	75-79 = 7
12 = 4	12 = 5	14 = 5	15 = 8	14 = 8	12 = 12	70-74 = 9
11 = 5	11 = 7	13 = 7	14 = 10	13 = 10	10 = 15	65-69 = 11
10 = 6	10 = 9	12 = 8	13 = 12	12 = 12	8 = 18	60-64 = 13
9 = 7	9 = 10	11 = 10	12 = 14	11 = 14	6 = 21	55-59 = 15
8 = 8	8 = 12	10 = 11	11 = 16	10 = 16	4 = 24	50-54 = 18
7 = 9	7 = 14	9 = 13	10 = 18	9 = 18	2 = 27	45-49 = 20
6 = 10	6 = 16	8 = 14	9 = 20	8 = 20	0 = 30	40-44 = 23
5 = 11	5 = 18	7 = 16	8 = 22	7 = 22		35-39 = 29
4 = 12	4 = 20	6 = 18	7 = 24	6 = 24		30-34 = 28
3 = 14	3 = 22	5 = 20	6 = 26	5 = 26		25-29 = 30
2 = 16	2 = 24	4 = 22	5 = 28	4 = 28		20-24 = 33
1 = 18	1 = 26	3 = 24	4 = 30	3 = 30		15-19 = 36
0 = 20	0 = 28	2 = 26	3 = 32	2 = 32		10-14 = 39
-1 = 22	-1 = 30	1 = 28	2 = 34	1 = 34		
-2 = 24	-2 = 32	0 = 30	1 = 36			
-3 = 26	-3 = 34	-1 = 32				
-4 = 30	-4 = 36	-2 = 34				
-5 = 32		-3 = 36				
-6 = 34						
-7 = 36						

Professional Jerry Tucker and referred to as "The Tucker 100 Test." The test takes about one hour to administer. Golfers hit shots and putts from specific distances, and their results are evaluated in the following skills: short putting, lag putting, chipping, pitching, greenside sand play and wedge play. Each skill is "scored," with points being awarded based on how close your shot finishes to the target (i.e., 3 points are earned if the ball finishes 4-6 feet from the hole). The scoring system gives golfers a "handicap" rating for each skill and an overall "Short Game Handicap." This test provides golfers and their coaches with reliable and useful feedback; it also serves as motivation for players to improve.

TOMI Computerized Putting Technique Evaluation

Marius Filmalter is a renowned putting researcher and instructor. He spent three years on the PGA Tour studying the technique and practice habits of the world's best putters. He has personally evaluated and coached Tiger Woods on putting. A native of South Africa, Filmalter has designed a computer software analysis system and putting training aid called TOMI, short for The Optimal Motion Instructor. TOMI is an infrared transmitter apparatus that is attached to a golfer's putter. The transmitter interfaces with a USB camera receiver connected to a computer.

I use the TOMI system with my students to gather valuable feedback about their putting strokes, including how they aim, their stroke path, tempo, contact point and angle of attack. Each golfer takes about 10 putts with a feedback clip attached to their putter. The feedback is powerful and useful for both the athlete and the coach since it cannot be seen with the naked eye. This type of computer feedback leads to improvement in a high percentage of cases.

TOMI STROKE CHART

Courtesy of TOMI

SELF-ANALYSIS TECHNIQUES

If you don't have access to this modern technology, then how do you evaluate your skills? You can still assess your skills the old-fashioned way. Accompanied by a friend, take your used balls (not range balls) onto your home course at a non-peak time. Measure out specific distances and set down temporary targets, such as a golf bag, opened umbrella, etc. Hit 10 balls with your normal full swing, and have your friend measure and record how far each shot flies. Average the results of the five best shots from each club. You'll soon be aware of how far each club flies (your carry yardages), and you'll know which clubs you need to practice, i.e., the ones with which you have the least control and confidence.

STATISTICAL ANALYSIS: FOUR THINGS TOP PERFORMERS HAVE IN COMMON

I've been very fortunate to call Peter Sanders a friend for

almost 20 years. The creator of ShotByShot.com, an online golf statistical analysis program, Peter has dedicated much of his adult life to the study of how golfers of all abilities get their ball into the hole. His website enables golfers to see what their handicap is in all facets of the game, relative to their target handicap group, and clearly identifies strengths and opportunities for improvement. The website draws on an incredible 150,000 rounds of golf in its data base.

A member of the prestigious *Golf Digest* Advisory Panel, Sanders contributes articles to the magazine regularly. He is also a consultant to several PGA and LPGA Tour players and more than 150 PGA teaching professionals nationwide, all of whom embrace ShotByShot.com. Here is some information that Peter has graciously shared with me over the years. It's made me a much better coach to my students, and I strongly encourage you to use it to your full advantage:

- *Greens in Regulation Percentage*: The most important and meaningful performance statistic in golf is Greens in Regulation or GIR. It's simple: The more greens you hit during the course of a round, the lower your score is likely to be. If you look at the leaderboard during most PGA Tour events, chances are that the leaders are also at or near the top in GIR percentage. Case in point: Winners on the PGA Tour hit about 12.5 GIR per round, or approximately 70 percent—this according to a profile of PGA Tour winners on ShotByShot.com. Money leader Luke Donald averaged 12 greens hit per round for the entire 2011 season (67%). Not surprisingly, he finished the year as the world's No. 1-ranked player and also captured Player of the

Year honors on both the PGA and European PGA Tours.

- *Tee shot Proficiency*: Most people think that the percentage of fairways you hit, or fairways in regulation (FIR), is highly correlated to performance. This is not always so. Both Tiger Woods and Luke Donald have achieved world No. 1 status by averaging only 64% FIR. However, in order to be a consistently elite competitive golfer, it's extremely important to put the ball in play consistently off the tee in a position where you can reasonably expect to hit the green in regulation. If you drive the ball into a water hazard, heavy rough or some other form of trouble, your chances of hitting the green on your next shot shrink substantially. According to research by ShotByShot.com, PGA Tour winners hit their tee shots into a position where they have "no shot" (requiring an advancement shot not directed at the green) only about once every 45 holes. Furthermore, they incur a one-shot penalty stroke (water or unplayable lie) as a result of an errant tee shot about once every 10 rounds, and they hit a wayward tee ball whereby they're penalized two strokes (lost ball or OB) only about once every 85 rounds. Great players may miss one-third of their fairways or more, but they're rarely out of position to hit a GIR and seldom ever penalized for a severe miscue.

- *Up-and-Down Percentage*: PGA Tour winners get the ball up-and-down approximately 70% of the time on shots within 50 yards of the hole. In addition, they make precious few short game errors in that

BREAKDOWN OF STROKES
+2 HANDICAP

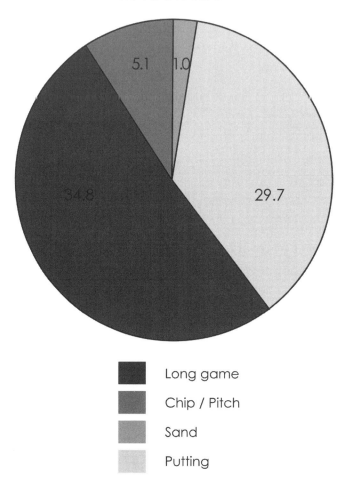

5.1   1.0

34.8

29.7

■ Long game

■ Chip / Pitch

■ Sand

■ Putting

Long Game Shots: 34.8
Chip/Pitch Shots: 5.1
Sand Shots: 1.0
Putts: 29.7
Average score: 71.6

they only miss the green about 6% of the time on their short game shots. A short game shot is any shot played from fairway or rough inside 50 yards. The message here is clear: To become an elite player, you need to develop a fantastic short game (a 70% conversion rate is sensational). You must also recognize those dangerous short game shots which can inflate your scores. When the situation warrants, play to a safe area on the green away from the hole; don't always try the heroic shot that can lead to a double bogey or worse.

- *3-Putt Percentage*: PGA Tour winners consistently make 70% or more of their putts in the 4- to 10-foot range. They also 3-Putt only 5% of the time in the 30- to 50-foot range. There's no question that if you want to be an elite competitive golfer, you need to become a tremendous putter and put in the necessary time and energy to develop this skill-set.

8

Conditioning, Nutrition and Hydration

"Tiger Woods showed [us] *what added strength, flexibility and improved conditioning—not to mention mental toughness—can do to improve one's game. He has inspired the entire golf community to recognize golf as an athletic sport."*

—Golf Fitness Magazine

Tiger Woods, Yani Tseng, Luke Donald and scores of golfers on the world's professional tours are dogged in their efforts to improve. They search for every conceivable edge they can, which includes being more physically fit than everyone else. The days when golfers were out of shape and mocked for their lack of athleticism are over as thousands of top amateur and professional golfers have committed themselves to golf-specific conditioning, nutrition and strength training programs.

Players today spend almost as much time in the gym as they do on the practice range. They often bring their own personal trainers to tournaments to help them stretch out and train before and after rounds. The top players understand that in order to play their best golf for 18 holes, day after day, they need to eat right, exercise, stay hydrated and get plenty of rest. A lapse in any one of these areas can lead to injury, a lack of stamina, increased mental mistakes and a poor attitude, all of which can impact their performance negatively.

Not every world class golfer is a physical specimen like Woods or Dustin Johnson, or has the nutritional discipline of, say, a Luke Donald. I'm sure there are a few glaring examples of unfit golfers that come to mind very quickly. But these people are outliers; you should not look to their example as being acceptable. The game is changing and quickly becoming a high performance sport. If you don't take your physical health and fitness seriously, you're likely to fall significantly behind your competition. But before you decide to commit yourself to a golf-specific conditioning program, you and your coach should consult a personal trainer or golf fitness specialist to construct a program that's right for you. While it's just as important to fine tune your body as it is your swing, one wrong turn can be devastating to your development and performance as a golfer.

In this chapter, I'll help you find the right fitness expert for you, debunk some common fitness myths and give you guidelines on the three primary elements of golf-specific training: strength, flexibility and endurance. And, since you are what you eat and drink, I'll provide you with some essential nutrition and hydration tips along with some pointers on how to get adequate amounts of rest.

How to Get Started

While being strong and fit has positive aspects that go beyond sport, strength training and conditioning is serious business. Training excessively or improperly can lead to injury and severely hinder your development. There's a lot of misinformation out there on strength training and conditioning, so it's important you seek out highly trained fitness professionals who do have the right information (i.e., those who have experience working with top-level golfers).

Athletes must consider three primary areas of training with regard to a golf-specific conditioning program: 1) strength; 2) flexibility; and 3) endurance. Each of these elements must be trained specific to golf if optimal performance is to be expected. Traditionally, strength training has been associated with sports such as football, hockey and wrestling where large muscular development is important. However, through the development of sport science in the last 30 years, exercise physiologists, coaches and athletes from many other sports have come to realize that strength training can help and not hinder performance.

Golf Fitness Education

To train correctly and get the best bang from your new found strength and endurance, make yourself aware of the various tools and services out there for the competitive golfer. The Titleist Performance Institute (TPI) based in Carlsbad, California is a leader in golf fitness education. Check out their website at mytpi.com for information about the best training methods and exercises for golfers, and then be sure to work with a fitness professional (in concert with your golf coach) who has expertise working with competitive golfers.

Strength Training

Everyone wants to get stronger so that they can generate more clubhead speed and distance. This is possible if you train properly and adhere to some guidelines. Remember: The ultimate goal is to shoot the lowest score possible. While it's tempting to look like a bodybuilder or football

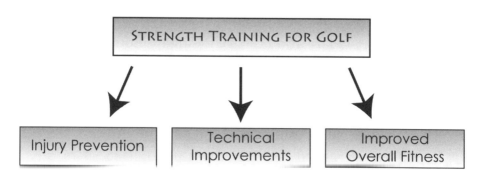

player, that should not be the goal for a high performance golfer.

One of the strongest golfers I know looks nothing like Dwayne "the Rock" Johnson. A few years ago, professional long driver Jeff Gavin visited me at the Titleist National Fitting Center at Eagles Nest Golf Club near Toronto. Jeff, with a camera crew from the Discovery Channel in tow, was trying to break the world record for initial ball speed off the clubface. He did so by generating 221 mph off ball speed with his 48-inch driver! His clubhead speed was 145 mph. To put that in perspective, Tiger Woods' average ball speed is about 180 mph and Bubba Watson's about 190 mph. When Gavin set the record, he drove the ball 408 yards (380 yards in the air). This occurred at sea level, on a calm day!

Gavin is the ultimate athlete when it comes to explosive power. But this 6-foot-3 former high jumper and triple jumper is lean, not bulky. His muscles are long and strong. He works out three times a week like a power lifter, using movements that train him to be as explosive as possible. Your golf-specific strength training program should also feature these "explosive" elements.

But be forewarned: If you try to bulk up too much too soon, or in the wrong manner, you could see a sharp decline in your game. I know a golfer who spent 10 or more hours a week in the gym, lifting weights. Unfortunately, his strength-training regimen was geared more toward playing football than golf. His bulked-up body looked good, but it didn't allow his swing to perform like it once did. As a result, his ball speed dropped from 165 mph to 155 mph, and he went from a slightly above-average power hitter to a short hitter at the NCAA Division I level. His performance dropped and he played his way off the travel team during his senior year.

Timing is another important part of strength training for golfers. Your regimen, like all of your other training, should follow the concept of periodization, i.e., doing specific things at specific times to facilitate peak performance in the most important competitions (see Chapter 5). The frequency and intensity of strength training will vary throughout the training year. For example, during the golf season, you'll be working to maintain the fitness level you've previously achieved, but along with fitting your conditioning into your schedule, you should follow the general guidelines for competitive golfers listed here:

1. Exercise selection. It's important to develop explosive power and train your muscles to be fast. There are many ways to do this whether you and your trainer choose exercises that mimic the swing or more general exercises adapted for a golfer. Mytpi.com has some excellent video examples of these more explosive, golf-specific exercises.

2. Frequency and recovery. The number of strength sessions per week will vary depending on your periodization model (3-4 times per week in the pre-competitive-season, 1-2 times per week in the competitive season). Recovery between strength-

training sessions will vary from 2-3 days depending on the phase of development.

3. In the gym, you should perform no more than 4-6 exercises per strength-training session, and should not exceed 30-36 total reps. The intensity should range between 60-90% of your maximum output, depending on the phase of the training year. You'll spend 2-3 minutes recovering between sets of the same exercise.

4. Injury prevention. The hips, shoulders, back and elbows are common trouble spots for golfers. A fitness professional can assess your weak areas and work to strengthen them to decrease your chances of injury.

5. Stabilization. The muscles that stabilize your core, upper and lower back, shoulders, elbows, wrists and ankles are key for high performance golfers and must be specifically trained.

6. Symmetry. It's common for the left and right sides of a golfer's body to develop significant differences in strength and balance. It's critical to correct the imbalance in the early part of the pre-competitive season, and to maintain balance throughout the year.

FOUR COMMON STRENGTH-TRAINING MYTHS

When developing your routine, keep in mind the four following misconceptions about strength training:

Myth 1: *Strength training for golf is the same as training for general fitness.*

Using bodybuilding methods to make your muscles larger can change your joint angles and compromise your swing mechanics. Bodybuilding helps isolate different muscle groups, while strength training for sport improves movement-specific strength and motor-pattern efficiency (i.e., a better kinematic sequence).

Myth 2: *Strength training will build huge muscles.*

Typical bodybuilding methods do lead to larger muscles, but strength training for golf makes muscles stronger, not necessarily larger. Golfers generally want to develop long, lean and powerful muscles—not tight and bulky ones.

Myth 3: *Strength training needs to be performed to exhaustion to be effective.*

Actually, strength training to "failure" negatively affects muscle development. Effective workouts for golfers do not generally cause soreness or stiffness afterwards.

Myth 4: *Strength training can be stopped once the season begins.*

You have to maintain any significant gains in strength during your competitive season. If you lose strength, you'll see a drop in performance and be more susceptible to injury. Most top golfers lessen their training frequency to two 45-minute sessions a week during the competitive season.

Flexibility

Flexibility is usually the most neglected part of an athlete's training program, and with top athletes, technical errors are often the result of inadequate flexibility. Correctly implemented, flexibility training can improve your performance. The key is to focus on improving your range of motion in areas crucial to the swing.

Those areas depend on your body, and you'll need a TPI Certified Golf Fitness Professional to tell you what you need to work on. But in general, the best golfers show a greater-than-average range of movement in all phases of the swing. They also have a more coordinated weight transfer during the backswing and forward swing leading to increased hip, shoulder and upper-body rotation. The result is a more coordinated sequence of movements, commonly referred to as an efficient "kinetic sequence," that allows for controlled power.

Lack of mobility in certain joints can reduce your ability to develop certain skills and lead to compromises or errors in your swing technique. For example, if you can't touch your toes because of poor hip mobility or hamstring inflexibility, you'll likely have difficulty getting into a good set-up posture and maintaining that posture throughout the swing.

It's also important to use flexibility training to balance your body. Differences in flexibility between your left and right sides can increase your risk of injury. Flexibility training should be done only for joints that are inflexible: Increasing flexibility in already healthy joints can create instability and increase the chance of injury.

You'll want to see a fitness specialist for a thorough evaluation and stretching plan, but keep in mind that he or she will likely introduce two methods to increase your flexibility: static and dynamic flexibility training. You have likely practiced static flexibility training as part of your post-game cool down. To perform a static stretch:

1. Slowly move the joint, or series of joints, to a stretching position.
2. Hold the stretch for 10-20 seconds, or until the tension releases.
3. Relax the muscles being stretched.
4. Re-stretch.

Static stretching should be implemented after each training session. A golfer should be stretching at least 3-6 days per week, holding each stretch for a total of 60 seconds. (Note: Completing four sets of 15 seconds is the same as doing three sets of 20 seconds.)

Dynamic—or ballistic flexibility training—on the other hand, is used in sports like golf that involve high-speed movement. Dynamic training uses repeated, fast movements, such as high kicks, to stretch the muscles and increase joint mobility. In a proper golf swing, energy is stored and then released through impact, creating enough momentum to carry the athlete's body through a full range of motion. Clubhead speeds can soar in excess of 115 mph; therefore, it's important that the elite golfer implement ballistic flexibility training into their workout routine.

Performing dynamic flexibility training during specific periods of the training cycle can improve your swing mechanics because it allows the body to move more freely through the entire range of motion, creating greater momentum and power. Dynamic flexibility conditioning for golf usually mimics the movement of the swing, progressively rotating the upper body and arms, then the lower body (i.e., hips), with increasing intensity. This movement is repeated for a specific number of sets and repetitions as set by your coach or trainer. The amount of training will vary from athlete to athlete, but the frequency is normally two days per week, with 3-4 days of rest between sessions.

Do not implement ballistic flexibility training into a young athlete's training schedule until a qualified physical trainer evaluates his or her readiness for this type of training, which includes running specific fitness tests on the athlete. Implementing ballistic training into the schedules of novice, untrained golfers who lack adequate strength, physical maturity or proper instruction can lead to injuries.

Flexibility and Skill Development

Great golfers are not robots who simply hit the same shot over and over again. Golf demands that the athlete train a range of different movement patterns to create a variety of different shots, depending on the situation at hand. Lack of flexibility in certain joints can greatly reduce a golfer's skill acquisition. If the athlete cannot achieve the range of movement required to reach a certain position in the swing, he will not execute the shot properly. The athlete's body will try to make some adjustments to compensate for this lack of flexibility. This, in turn, will lead to poor swing mechanics, reduced power and a loss of control.

Having an optimal amount of flexibility, especially in the shoulders, upper torso and hips, facilitates an efficient kinematic sequence (more on this shortly) and allows the clubhead to reach maximum speed. This clubhead speed helps determine the distance the ball will travel, how much it will spin and its trajectory. All golfers should strive to hit the ball with a square clubface (toward their intended target) with maximum force. This is what the top players do.

FOUR FLEXIBILITY TRAINING MYTHS

Myth 1: *Static stretching is the only way to improve a golfer's flexibility.*

For someone just starting flexibility training, static stretching is a safe and effective way to increase general flexibility; however, dynamic flexibility training is better at increasing the range of motion your body needs to generate maximum clubhead speed.

Myth 2: *Stretching before a round prevents injuries.*

Stretching helps the athlete to prepare his body to move efficiently and powerfully in competition. Every golfer should have pre- and post-round stretching regimens; however, most injuries are not caused by poor flexibility, but by weakness or strength issues or overuse/overtraining.

Myth 3: *Strength, not flexibility, helps you drive the ball farther.*

A golfer needs the combination of both strength and flexibility to perform his best. The swing is a coordinated sequence of movements; chronically tight muscles cause compensations during the swing and lead to a less-than-optimal kinetic sequence.

Myth 4: *Flexibility training can be stopped once the season begins.*

Any gain in flexibility will be lost if it's not maintained during the competitive season. Golfers are encouraged to stretch daily year round. Many top-level players find yoga to be beneficial to their performance and career longevity.

THE KINEMATIC SEQUENCE

Establishing sound body positioning at address gives you the ability to generate maximum clubhead speed at impact. The backswing creates energy, which increases throughout the swing motion and is eventually delivered to the ball. This storing and transferring of energy is commonly referred to as the "kinematic sequence." An efficient kinetic sequence makes the golf swing look effortless yet extremely powerful. This is due mainly to the optimal coordination of the muscles involved in the swing, and the synchronizing of rotational speeds. The more prepared these

171

KINEMATIC SEQUENCE

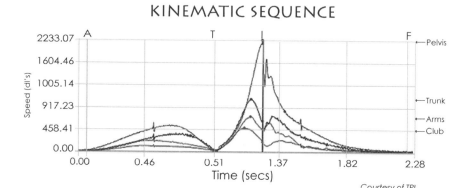

Courtesy of TPI

muscles are at dealing with the physical demands of the game, the better the athlete's performance is likely to be.

Modern 3D video technology is becoming more and more prevalent in high-performance golf testing and training. It's used extensively at TPI and other golf swing research centers. Three dimensional motion capture system technology creates a 3D image, or likeness, of your golf swing, and measures the rotational movements and speeds of different parts of your body and the club. The findings are plotted onto a graph compared to optimal sequencing patterns. Coaches can use the data to pinpoint key areas to be improved upon in the athlete's swing, like an MRI machine for coaches. The video measures and evaluates the swing motion in ways that the naked eye or traditional 2D video cannot.

Coaches at TPI use 3D graphs to measure and evaluate body positions and rotational speeds during the backswing, transition, downswing and follow-through. The area of interest for this research is primarily the downswing, but includes aspects of the transition and follow-through.

Endurance Training

Walking the course to develop your aerobic fitness is like thoughtlessly hitting buckets of balls to improve your swing:

Your performance will only reach the level of your effort. You don't need to be as fit as Lance Armstrong, but you should be healthy enough to play four rounds of competitive golf without tiring. Golfers walk an average of four to five miles per round. If you're not fit, over the course of a tournament you can experience fatigue, a loss of concentration and poor decision-making.

Soreness and fatigue result from a buildup of lactic acid in your muscles. Lactic acid is what causes the burning sensation you feel during intense activity. Some golfers can have lactate levels of 3.0-5.0 even when walking 2-1/2 to 3 mph. These levels, prolonged over the course of a round or tournament, cause progressive fatigue. On the course, it's possible to experience a slow, imperceptible buildup of lactic acid called lactic creep. There's no burning sensation, but it's a game-killer nonetheless. Over the course of 18 holes, swing mechanics and mental awareness can be significantly compromised.

Golfers should perform 30 to 45 minutes of aerobic exercise three to five times a week during the off-season, and two to four days a week during the competitive season. This is the best way to keep your fitness level above the demands of the sport and to mitigate the likelihood of performance drops due to the effects of lactic acid buildup.

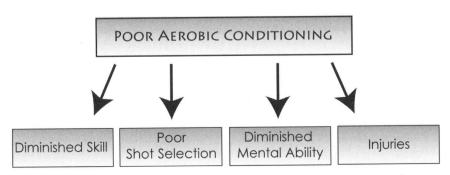

ENDURANCE MODEL

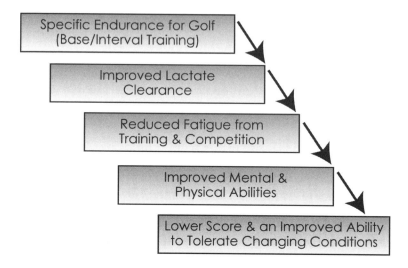

To improve your endurance, think of your training as an aerobic training progression.

Frequency: three to five days per week during the off-season, one to two days per week during the competitive season. Aerobic activities can include light jogging, riding a bike or training on a treadmill.

Duration: 30 or more minutes per session.

Intensity: To be determined by lactate testing, with specific interval training intensities as determined by lactate testing. Interval training involves interspersing bursts of high-intensity work (such as sprinting on a treadmill or biking really fast) with periods of low-intensity work (i.e., walking on a treadmill, biking slow).

THREE ENDURANCE TRAINING MYTHS

Myth 1: *Playing golf will improve aerobic fitness to required levels.*

Playing golf will increase your aerobic fitness, but only to the level experienced during a typical round. If you're required to walk farther, or to play on a hilly course, you'll wind up fatigued. The higher you push your fitness level above what you need to play golf, the less fatigue you'll experience during competitive rounds.

Myth 2: *Aerobic fitness will cause muscle fatigue that interferes with skill development.*

When performed at the proper intensity (as determined by a fitness professional), aerobic training doesn't interfere with skill development.

Myth 3: *Aerobic training can be stopped once the season begins.*

You have to maintain your aerobic fitness during the competitive season. If it's lost, your performance will suffer. Generally, 30-45 minutes of cardio training two to four times a week will maintain fitness.

NUTRITION FOR GOLF

Most players are aware that a good diet is essential to good health; however, not everyone is aware of how much your diet can affect your ability to meet mental and physical challenges during competition. Nutrition advice is complex and often contradictory. Dr. Deborah Graham, a sports psychologist who founded GolfPsych, and Joanne Flynn, a registered nutritionist, have researched nutrition for golfers and found a direct link between optimum nutrition and success on the course (see accompanying chart). From their research, Dr. Flynn came up with the following nine nutrition tips to help golfers reach their maximum performance state on the course.

NUTRITION FOR GOLF

Optimum Nutrition → Optimum Brain & Body Function → Strokes Off Your Game

The Front 9 of Nutrition

HOLE 1

Don't bogey breakfast. Studies indicate that breakfast-eaters perform better. An ideal breakfast would consist of protein (skim milk, eggs, yogurt, peanut butter) and complex carbohydrates (eggs and steel cut oatmeal).

HOLE 2

Tea it up. Make the cut by eliminating coffee. Coffee can cause carb and sugar cravings, low energy and decreased focus. Green tea gives you Vitamin C, as well as cancer-fighting properties.

HOLE 3

Don't "slice" it. With white bread, that is! Enriched flour has sugar, and sugar causes low energy and decreased focus. Switch from refined grains to whole grains such as brown rice, oatmeal and whole wheat.

HOLE 4

Power up with protein. Eating protein improves your lean muscle mass, concentration, immunity and energy. Good sources of protein include lean meats and poultry, fish, eggs, nuts, seeds and legumes. You need between .8 and 1.2 grams per pound of body weight per day. So, for a 200-pound athlete, that's 160-240 grams. Women who eat three meals a day need 30-40 grams per meal, about one-palm sized portion. Men need 50-60 grams per meal, about two palm-sized portions.

HOLE 5

Eat your "greens." Greens and other colorful foods, like beets (Fruit Loops don't count!), have anti-aging properties. The top three green foods are spinach, kale and broccoli.

HOLE 6

Skip the junk. Foods consisting of refined carbs and saturated or trans fats lead to low energy, impaired focus, weight gain and poor athletic performance.

HOLE 7

Eat like a shark. Try to eat plenty of fish, which are full of healthy amounts of omega-3 fatty acids. These acids lead to optimum brain, cellular (energy) and heart function. Other sources include nuts, seeds and eggs.

HOLE 8

Pack your 15th club. While you can't play without a putter, it's just as important to put some healthy snacks in your bag, such as almonds, walnuts, berries, seeds, low-sugar protein bars and low-fat cheese.

HOLE 9

Don't become a water hazard. The benefits of keeping hydrated include fat metabolism, proper muscle and skin tone, and more energy. Drink a minimum of 10 glasses per day and avoid sugary sports drinks.

PRE–ROUND NUTRITION

It's critical to eat a proper meal before you tee it up.

Eating before a round enables you to maintain appropriate blood sugar levels, and therefore maximize abilities to manage concentration, relaxation and emotional stability while playing.

Pre–Round Challenges

Various Tee Times: When teeing off at 7 a.m., it may be difficult to find the time, the right foods or the appetite to eat. With an 11 a.m. tee time, 10 a.m. might feel too late for breakfast but too early for lunch.

Suggestion: Change your mealtime to within two hours of your tee time to give you sustained energy throughout the round. For best results, make the meal a balance of complex or slow-release carbohydrates and protein. A meal consisting of eggs, whole-wheat toast and fresh fruit will give you greater sustained energy than pancakes with syrup and orange juice. Pack nutritious snacks for the course, such as mixed nuts, trail mix, fruits (fresh and dried), cheese sticks and peanut butter sandwiches. You should be eating regularly on the course to maintain energy levels.

Pre-Round Jitters: Many players feel that if they eat before a round, they will not be able to "keep it down." By choosing not to eat, they sacrifice muscle coordination, mental acuity, patience and stamina.

Suggestion: Opt for a nutritious drink instead of a meal. There are many ready-to-mix protein drinks and powders that can be blended or shaken into an easy-to-digest meal. Most of these drinks provide a good balance of protein, carbohydrates and fats to keep you mentally sharp. Two–time U.S. Open Champion Lee Janzen and many others on the PGA Tour travel with a small blender and protein powder so that they can prepare fresh fruit and protein drinks before they play.

Expediency and Lack of Planning: Some players choose to dismiss the importance of nutrition. They grab whatever they can before, during and after rounds. This makes it unlikely that the player will find food with suitable nutritional value.

Suggestion: Pack sports bars like BALANCE or MET-Rx and eat them whenever suitable food isn't available.

ACTIVE PLAYING NUTRITION

Experiment with snacks and foods to eat on the course to find the best combinations for you. With sports bars, remember that the ones that don't taste very good often provide the best nutrition. If you feel the need for some quick energy while playing, you may want to try healthy, "fast-release" foods such as bananas, dates, apricots, bagels, whole wheat pretzels, crackers or sweetened yogurt. If you're looking for more sustained energy, you should consider eating "slow-release" foods such as apples, grapes, nuts, pears, popcorn, cheese or unsweetened yogurt.

THE RIGHT NUTRITION BAR FOR YOU

Keeping your blood sugar level helps prevent fatigue, allowing you to achieve peak energy levels and maintain focus on the course. Food bars can provide a quick, convenient and nutritious snack during a round of golf. There are many choices to choose from including high protein and low carb options. Which should you choose? Dr. Robert Yang, co–founder of the Pure Performance Clinic and a consultant to the Titleist

Performance Institute, says you should base your decision on the quality of the ingredients. Here are a few other factors to consider, according to Dr. Yang:

- "Less is more" when it comes to the number of ingredients. Bars with 10-15 ingredients are your best option.
- Choose an organic bar. Your body won't have to detoxify residues of pesticides and herbicides, which are neurotoxins and/or hormone disrupters.
- Look for minimal processing, meaning the bar has not been heated beyond 105 degrees. This ensures that the fats and proteins have not been denatured. Both organic and minimally processed whole-food bars have healthy fats, moderate protein levels, and slow digesting carbohydrates, which should ensure stable blood sugar levels throughout your round.

KEEPING HYDRATED

Perhaps the most important thing that you can do for yourself while playing is to keep yourself adequately hydrated. Even on cool days, the wind and sun will dehydrate the body through perspiration and respiration. Moderate dehydration can reduce physical stamina making it harder to control muscles and maintain energy throughout the round. Moderate dehydration can also cause you to lose your mental stamina and your ability to think around the course. Decision-making can become impaired and much less effective. More serious symptoms of dehydration can include headaches, lightheadedness, impaired memory and difficulty breathing. Tour players and their caddies find it very helpful to drink, on average, about a half-cup of water per hole to ensure that mental and physical skills are not compromised by dehydration. Alcohol and caffeine (found in coffee and many soft drinks) increase rates of dehydration. Committed athletes refrain from both while in competition.

More on Hydration

Hydration is a key component of performance that is often overlooked by athletes and coaches. It's critical to be adequately hydrated for optimal body function and motor-skill performance. During practice and play, golfers lose large amounts of water, vital minerals and electrolytes. In the summer months, you can lose as much as two percent of your total body weight. Even on cold days, physical activity can cause dehydration.

Dr. Yang suggests that the optimal amount of water is half your body weight (in pounds) in ounces per day. For example, a 200-pound person needs to drink 100 ounces of water per day. A key point to remember is that other fluids—including coffee, tea, juice, soda, milk, sports drinks, and flavored water—do not count toward this total. In fact, sports drinks and juices can actually dehydrate the body because water is needed to dilute the high amount of sugar assimilated into the body.

The timing of water consumption is also very important to optimal hydration, according to Dr. Yang. Drinking water first thing in the morning is essential because the body becomes dehydrated during sleep. Start with 25 percent of your total water intake in the morning. If your water intake for the day is 100 ounces, consume 25 ounces in the early hours. During a round of golf, you should consume 40-50 percent of your total daily intake of water; therefore, if your water intake for the day is 100 ounces, consume 40-50 ounces on the course. The remaining water should be consumed throughout the day.

PLANE SPEAKING

If you're traveling to a tournament by airplane, be sure to drink four to eight ounces of water per hour that you're in the air. Airplane air is incredibly dry, and you don't want to get dehydrated before you hit your first shot.

SYMPTOMS OF DEHYDRATION

According to the International Sports Medicine Institute, most athletes are dehydrated before they begin to play or practice, because they haven't had enough water to drink. The following are common signs of mild dehydration:

1. Flushed face
2. Extreme thirst
3. Dry, warm skin
4. Small amounts of dark yellow urine
5. Dry lips with thick saliva
6. Moderate physical fatigue or weakness
7. Mild muscle cramping in arms and legs
8. Mild headache
9. Difficulty concentrating
10. Poor mental routine
11. Indecision
12. Increased irritability, anger
13. Easily frustrated

When you're active for more than one hour, you lose electrolytes as well as water. If your sweat burns your eyes, or if it leaves white marks on your hat or shirt, it's evidence of a high electrolyte loss. It's important that these electrolytes be replaced for two key reasons: First, your body will not effectively retain the water you drink if electrolytes are also not replaced. Thus, players who drink water all the time can still be dehydrated. Second, a healthy balance of water and electrolytes is vital to your bodily functions.

In order to stay hydrated for competitive golf, you should obey the following guidelines:

1. Drink water at least 60 minutes before play or practice because by the time you feel thirsty, you'll already be dehydrated.
2. Drink every 15 minutes during play, and then following play.
3. Drink small quantities frequently to minimize stomach discomfort.
4. Salt your food with unprocessed salt, like sea salt, which can be found in most gourmet groceries or health food stores. It has more natural minerals and less iodine than processed salt. (Contrary to popular belief, you do need some salt!)
5. Avoid soft drinks, which can facilitate dehydration.
6. Choose a drink that has all of the important electrolytes and minerals. Be careful of common sports drinks that are laced with sugar, which can spike arousal levels and hamper water absorption. These popular drinks ideally should be diluted about 3:1 with water. Electrolyte replacement drinks can be found in health stores. These drinks do not need to be diluted.

ILLEGAL SUBSTANCES IN GOLF

Golf is now part of the world-wide movement in sport

HYDRATION CHECK

A simple way to determine your hydration status is to weigh yourself before exercise, practice and play, then weigh yourself again afterwards. For every pound lost, you need to drink 20-24 ounces of fluid, preferably an electrolyte drink such as Back Nine Lytes or Pedialyte.

---

to institute random drug testing to ensure the integrity of competition. The International Golf Federation (IGF) began random drug testing at the World Amateur Team Championship in 2006 in South Africa. The IGF uses the World Anti-Doping Agency (WADA) drug testing methods and protocols just like all of the Olympic sports. Athletes and coaches are informed and trained concerning these rules, which can be found online at internationalgolffederation.org. A banned substances list, other rules and answers to Frequently Asked Questions are available through WADA.

In 2008, the PGA Tour mandated its members to follow WADA regulations, in part to help facilitate golf's successful bid to become a competitive sport at the 2016 Summer Olympic Games in Brazil. Other professional tours around the globe are doing the same. Collegiate golfers must follow the NCAA drug and anti- doping rules. College athletes are subject to random testing, and are made aware of these rules and testing procedures by athletic department leaders at mandatory training and information workshops conducted annually.

SLEEP AND REST TIPS

Many aspiring competitive golfers aren't aware of how much rest and sleep can affect their performance and skill development. In order to play and improve to the best of your ability, you should:

1. Get eight-plus hours of quality sleep per night.
2. Do your best to go to sleep and wake up at the same times each day.
3. When necessary, rest or nap for 60-90 minutes maximum during the day. Set an alarm so that you don't sleep longer, and never nap after 5:00 p.m.
4. When changing time zones, get into the rhythm of the new time zone immediately and go to bed at your normal bed time, if possible.
5. Listen to your body—take breaks when they're needed to guard against burnout.

9

Clubfitting: Discovering the Best Equipment for You

"Touring pros play fitted equipment, no matter which brand sponsors them. Poorly fitted clubs will punish a good swing with a bad shot. Properly fitted clubs reward good swings with good shots."

—Peter Jacobsen, Champions Tour Player and TV Commentator

Equipment is an important variable that's under your control. Playing equipment that's correctly fitted to your body and swing will make you a better player. It's imperative that your clubs work with you, not against you. You should never be forced into adjusting your fundamentals and compromising your swing technique for the sake of making your clubs work. Your clubs should perform as designed and feel right when you make a sound, balanced swing.

Most golfers are understandably confused when seeking new equipment. Manufacturers' marketing claims are often erroneous, and the various technologies can be a bit overwhelming. There are many new products on the market and all claim to be the best for you. Incredulous promises are commonplace. Some infomercials are misleading to the point of being outrageous, and the jargon is often difficult to grasp. Furthermore, the salespeople in retail stores seldom have the proper equipment or expertise to serve your needs as a competitive golfer. It's very easy to walk into a store and buy clubs off the rack. Don't succumb to this temptation. You'll be much better off exhibiting patience and having your clubs custom fit by a trained PGA Professional.

If your equipment is properly fitted to you, you'll feel confident that each club will perform as desired when you execute the correct swing technique. You should feel excited about your equipment and like the way your clubs look and feel. You should also expect your clubs to control the distance, trajectory and spin of your shots better. You're likely to hit more good shots with fitted clubs, maximizing distance, optimizing trajectory and producing a tighter overall dispersion pattern.

In this chapter, you'll learn how to select the best equipment and ball for you. You'll also learn about the latest technology and trends in custom fitting, how the process works and how to find an expert fitter in your area.

Get Fit

Make sure you have your equipment fitted by a trained PGA Professional or certified fitter. Scores of PGA Professionals at public and private courses and practice facilities have the expertise and equipment to conduct a fitting session. Many club manufacturers also have their own testing facilities where you can be fitted by one of their trained specialists. To find someone who specializes in custom fitting near you, contact your local PGA section office or visit the websites of the major equipment manufacturers. You can also ask for word-of-mouth references from the top competitive golfers or equipment sales reps in your area.

What to Expect From a Fitting Session

Clubfitting is not an exact science, although it's much better than ordering clubs online or buying them off eBay. Most fitters today will put you on TrackMan or some other launch monitor system, which precisely measures impact conditions, shot performance and other critical ball flight data. Different golf ball, shaft and clubhead combinations can be compared and evaluated using these systems, so that you and your fitter can make informed choices.

Most fitting professionals charge a fee equal to their hourly rate for instruction, although some waive the fee if the customer places an order for a set of clubs. Aside from the fee, most custom-fitted equipment costs the same as off-the-rack clubs. There are exceptions, however, especially if you go with a custom upgrade for a shaft and not the manufacturer's stock offering. It takes about two to three hours for a full-bag fitting, and about an hour each for a putter, iron or driver fitting. Most manufacturers will deliver your clubs in 7-10 days after you place your order.

A fitting session is usually an enjoyable and enlightening experience. You should arrive at least 15 minutes early to warm up. Wear your usual golf attire, including shoes, glove, hat and, if the fitting is outdoors, sunscreen. Also make sure to bring your current set of clubs so that the fitter can measure them for lie, loft, length, shaft flex, etc. You should expect to hit a few balls with your old clubs so that the fitter can get a baseline to compare with the test clubs he selects. Have an open mind and follow the directions provided by your fitting professional. Ask questions if you're confused or uncertain about the fitting terminology and the data being collected off the launch monitor. You're likely to be exposed to information and ideas that you haven't heard before.

Static Fitting Versus Dynamic Fitting

In a static fitting, the fitter takes your physical measurements (height, wrist to floor, hand size, etc.), maybe has you make a few swings on a lie board, and then uses this information to recommend a set of clubs for you. This is unadvisable; so, too, is hitting ball after ball indoors into a net with or without calibrated machines. The fitters who do this for a living are generally well-intentioned; however, your new equipment needs to be tested in the same environment in which it'll be used— that is, outdoors, where full ball flight can be observed.

The latter is called a dynamic fitting because you're actively participating by hitting shots on a practice range (or from a hitting bay to a range) under the watchful eye of a trained PGA Professional or professional club fitter. In these conditions, the fitter can observe the complete flight of the ball, the impact conditions (i.e., divot patterns), and your "real" swing tendencies. In most cases, your fitter will also be using TrackMan or some other launch monitor device to measure important ball flight and impact data, such as spin rate, clubhead speed, ball speed, launch angle, dispersion (i.e., the direction your shots travel, and how tightly clustered your misses are), carry distance and landing angle. This information is used by the fitter, in conjunction with what he's observing with his own eyes, to give you the best club fitting experience possible.

The fitting process is a very enlightening experience for most golfers. It enables the discovery of golf equipment to take place. Each club is suited to the player in every way—length, lie angle, shaft flex, shaft composition, grip size, head design. The golf professional facilitates the fitting process by leading you through the various steps necessary to determine which clubs perform best for you. The professional provides you with information, feedback and suggestions. This enables you to make educated choices when selecting your equipment. The fitting process is not about a professional telling you what you need but rather, it's an opportunity for you to select equipment that looks appealing and is suitable to play with.

A Step-by-Step Approach to Clubfitting

A trained golf professional will follow a systematic approach to fitting as outlined in the sections below. They'll help you determine your optimal equipment specifications by leading you through this step-by-step approach. When the session is completed, it's likely that you'll have the knowledge and confidence to make the most prudent decisions regarding your equipment.

STEP 1: Choose Your Ball First

The first and arguably most important step in the custom fitting process is to discover the best golf ball for you and your game because it will be in play for all of your shots. How far the ball goes, how quickly it stops, how much it curves, and how it performs in different weather conditions will all have a direct impact on your score. You must have confidence in the ball you use under tournament conditions. It's important not to choose a ball that simply travels the farthest, but rather one that gives you the best combination of distance, trajectory control, spin and feel.

To find the right ball, experiment with what the Tour players use. Try several different top line balls to see how they fly, feel and react in different course and weather conditions. Then, when you think you've found a ball that best performs for you, do your homework: Read the ball design characteristics (ball speed, spin rate, and cover composition) on the manufacturer's website, and make sure that your choice is designed for a player with your clubhead speed and needs. It may be that you drive the ball great, but struggle around the greens. In this instance, you may be better suited playing a ball that spins more around the greens and has good stopping power. Consult with your coach to confirm that your choice is a sound one. Once you've committed to a ball, you can test equipment to see what makes your ball perform best.

STEP 2: Get Your Irons Fitted for Length

Determining the best club length for you is the first step in the iron-fitting process. The length of your clubs affects how solidly you strike the ball and how far it travels. The correct length should allow you to assume the best possible athletic posture at address, and help you remain there throughout the swing. If correct, you should be able to swing naturally and powerfully into a balanced finish, and hit consistently solid shots without having to compensate your swing technique

Golf professionals generally test golfers for length with a system devised by equipment manufacturers. You'll be asked to hit several 6-irons of different lengths because this club has an appropriate amount of loft and spin to provide reliable feedback. Mis-hits will be obvious, not only by feel, but because the clubface is taped to show where the ball has made contact on the face (see page 193). The professional will help you to discover your optimal club length by evaluating these impact marks, as well as observing ball flight, swing technique, posture and balance. TrackMan (or the launch monitor utilized) will compare and contrast your performance with all test clubs by measuring ball speed, launch angle, spin rate, shot dispersion, carry distance and other vital statistics. This testing procedure, with the guidance of a trained fitting professional, will make it easy to determine the optimal length for your clubs.

IDEAL CLUB LENGTH

too short   ideal   too long

The middle club gives the golfer the best possibility to make sweet spot contact. Although playing with clubs that are slightly longer or shorter than your ideal length (plus or minus 1/4"-1/2") might seem insignificant, it can have far-reaching consequences.

STEP 3: Determine the Lie Angle

Once the club's length is determined, you can fit for the appropriate lie angle. The lie angle is the angle (measured in degrees) formed between the centerline of the shaft and the ground when the club is soled in a neutral position. It can have a great influence on both the ball's direction and distance.

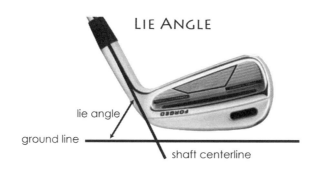

LIE ANGLE

lie angle

ground line

shaft centerline

To determine the optimal lie angle, a professional tapes the bottom of the club before you hit from a "lie board." The professional can then observe marks on the bottom of the club (see below). The fitter presents different lie angle possibilities until the best one is found.

IDEAL LIE ANGLE

left of target   straight flight   right of target

too upright   ideal   too flat

It's common for golfers to play with lie angles that are off by two degrees or more. As a result, these players have to modify their technique to make the clubs work. This is one reason why some people develop unorthodox swings. Research by Titleist shows that a lie angle that's two degrees off on a 165-yard 6-iron shot causes the ball to fly 20 feet (approximately 7 yards) off-line, and a 4-degree difference causes it to fly 40 feet off-line.

Ideally, you should use irons that strike the turf squarely after contact. If the toe strikes the turf first, the lie angle is too upright and the ball will tend to fly to the left; and if the heel of the club contacts the turf first, the lie is too flat and the ball will fly to the right. When the club strikes the turf squarely, the ball has the greatest chance of flying directly toward the target (see illustrations above). Professional fitters equipped with TrackMan or the like can easily help you discover the optimal lie angles for your clubs through testing and evaluation.

STEP 4: Choose a Shaft Flex

The next step is to discover the best shaft option—weight, flex and torque—for your irons and woods. Work with your fitting professional to test and discover a shaft that is designed to be a good match with your ball speed and club delivery patterns (i.e., the angle of attack—ascending or descending—the clubhead takes into the ball), and one that feels good and produces a desirable ball flight. Play shafts that are engineered to perform for your strength and swing patterns.

SHAFT COMPOSITION—GRAPHITE OR STEEL?

Many golfers are uncertain whether they should use graphite or steel shafts. Most top golfers choose steel for their irons and graphite or exotic shafts for their driver, fairway metals and hybrids. There are quite a few differences between the two, as outlined here, although they may not be as significant as they were once thought to be.

Steel Shafts

- Very consistent in flex from shaft to shaft.
- More reliable consistency than graphite.
- Easier to manufacture, and therefore less expensive than graphite.
- Heavier at lower flexes (regular, medium and stiff flexes) than graphite.
- Perform reliably at all speeds, i.e., ball flight and distance control can be controlled on partial shots.

- Have a lower launch trajectory and spin rate than graphite, thus produce a more penetrating ball flight.
- Can be manufactured with shock-dampening properties.

Graphite Shafts

- Considerably lighter than steel at lower flexes. Most people will hit graphite-shafted clubs farther than steel because they can swing them faster and launch them higher.
- Designed to perform optimally at "all out" speed; thus, professionals often choose graphite for drivers and fairway metals. Ball flight tends to "balloon" when high-speed players hit finesse or specialty shots, especially into the wind.
- Manufactured with heavier heads than their steel counterparts to balance the weight ratio of the components.

GRIP SIZE AND STYLE

The thickness or diameter of a player's grips is very important and often overlooked. Grip size is based on personal preference and is usually correlated to hand size. (The fitter will use a chart to measure and recommend the appropriate grip size.) Grip diameter can be easily altered by switching to correct-size grips or by adding or subtracting the amount of tape under the grip. Some grip types are more durable than others. Choose a grip that appeals to you and check with your fitting professional to make sure it's a recommended selection.

CLUBHEAD DESIGN

Select a clubhead design that reflects your skill level and the ball flight characteristics that you desire. As a competitive player, you'll be understandably interested and attracted to high-performance "better player's clubs," not game-improvement clubs. You're looking in the correct category, but don't select clubheads because they're the latest "it" model or your favorite Tour player uses them. Be sure to select clubs that are exciting for you to play but are also engineered to match the swing and game that you have now. Make sure that your clubs have the appropriate amount of loft and offset, and that the center of gravity location best matches your preferred launch. Follow the recommendations and guidance offered by your fitting professional.

SET COMPOSITION:
WHAT CLUBS SHOULD YOU HAVE IN THE BAG?

You must be able to hit all of your clubs with a playable trajectory, meaning that you can control the ball and stop it on the green. Your fitting professional can help you decide whether your iron set composition should be 3-iron through pitching wedge (PW), 4 through PW, or 5 through PW. Once you have determined your iron set composition, you can make sound choices regarding fairway metals, hybrids and wedges. Some common combinations are:

- 4-PW; 19-degree hybrid; 54- and 58-degree wedges; 3- and 5-woods; driver; putter
- 4-PW; 17-degree hybrid; 52-, 56- and 60-degree wedges; 3-wood; driver; putter
- 5-PW; 54- and 58-degree wedges; 3-, 5-, 7- and 9-woods; driver; putter

DRIVER FITTING

You need a driver you can hit consistently with as much distance and accuracy as possible. Ideally, your driver should have a launch angle (i.e., "take-off" trajectory) of 10-14 degrees and a spin rate of 2,200-3,000 rpm (revolutions per minute) so that it will roll effectively to maximize distance (see the illustration below). TrackMan can measure driver performance and compare performance patterns with optimal possibilities for the golfer given his clubhead speed and swing delivery pattern.

Like your irons, your driver should be the optimal length to ensure consistent sweet spot contact. Many people hit the ball farther and more accurately with drivers shorter than the standard 45 inches. This process to determine the correct length is essentially the same as it is for irons.

OPTIMUM BALL FLIGHT

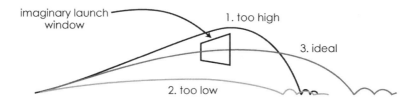

WEDGE FITTING

Your fitting professional will use the loft of your pitching wedge, as well as the other clubs in your bag, as a starting point to determine what additional wedges you'll need. Your wedges should ideally be 4-6 degrees apart in loft to minimize yardage gaps. In addition, the sole designs should complement your game, enabling you to hit all of the shots you'll encounter—chips, pitches, lobs, bunker shots, and other specialty shots.

APPROXIMATE SPIN RATE CHANGE VS. IMPACT POINT (IN RPM)

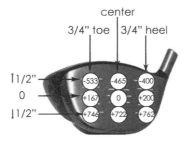

Your fitting professional will observe your technique and tendencies before recommending possibilities. Players who are "diggers," i.e., hit down on the ball sharply and take a divot, usually perform best with higher-bounce angles. Sweepers and sliders, i.e., players who take little or no turf with their wedges, usually play their best with lower bounce angles.

BOUNCE ANGLE

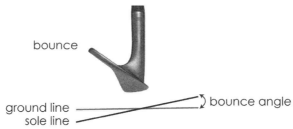

The bounce angle is the curvature of the sole measured from the leading edge to the trailing edge.

PUTTER FITTING

Putts account for about 40% of all strokes taken in a round of golf and yet, until recently, putter fittings have lagged significantly behind iron and driver/fairway metal fittings. A high percentage of golfers play with putters that are generally too long and force them to compromise their fundamentals and technique. A proper-length putter should connect the distance from where the eyes hit the ground to where the arms hang naturally under the shoulders. This enables the golfer to develop sound putting mechanics and aim, and gain a true perspective over their putts.

A good friend of mine, Todd Sones, Top 100 Teacher and renowned putting coach and designer from Chicago, uses the Pythagorean theorem (A2 + B2 = C2) to help golfers determine their optimal putter length. He's seen many of his students improve their performance simply by using the correct length putter. Sones' method is as follows:

THE GEOMETRY OF GOLF
Find The Optimal Length Of Your Putter Using the Pythagorean Theorem (A2 + B2=C2)

STEP 1: Set up in the proper posture as illustrated.

STEP 2: To determine measurement A (the vertical leg of the triangle), measure the distance from your top wrist crease down to the ground.

STEP 3: To measure B (the horizontal line of the triangle), place a mirror on the ground on the target line. Set up with your eyes over the ball (see your eyes in the mirror) then measure the distance of a line from your toes to the center of the ball.

STEP 4: Once the vertical leg (A) and horizontal leg (B) of the triangle have been determined, then square them and add them together, following the Pythagorean theorem ($A^2 + B^2 = C^2$) to calculate C2. Then you need to figure out the square

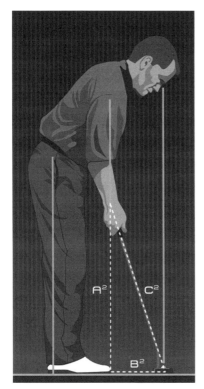

root of C (a good calculator or square root calculator website can help you do this) to find the measurement of the diagonal leg of the triangle, and your optimal putter length. For example, if your wrist to ground measurement is 32" (A) and your toes to golf ball measurement is 9" (B), then your optimal putter length is 33.25"—(A2 = 32 x 32 = 1,024") + (B2 = 9 x 9 = 81) = (C2 = 1,105 = 33.25").

GROOVE, GRIP WEAR

You should consider replacing your wedges every year, since the grooves wear down and lose effectiveness with use. You should also change your grips at least once a year and have someone check the lofts and lie angles of your irons before the start of each season and at the beginning of the competitive season (as they can shift over time with intense practice and play).

COMMON EQUIPMENT MYTHS AND PITFALLS TO AVOID

- Don't buy knock-off clubs. They may look top-notch, but they will not perform as such. These clubs are manufactured with inferior materials and workmanship. In many cases, the lofts, sweet spots, swing weights, centers of gravity, etc., are inconsistent and unacceptable. If you're searching for bargain prices on top equipment, your golf professional may know of some excellent trade-in sets.

- Never cut down or add length to a club. This destroys the swing weight (balance) of the club, and alters the shaft flex and effective lie angle.

- Clubheads manufactured for graphite shafts must always have graphite shafts. Never take a graphite-shafted club and switch to a steel shaft, or vice versa. The clubheads are specially weighted to perform with a specific shaft type. Clubheads manufactured for graphite shafts are heavier than those designed for steel shafts to accommodate for the lightness of the shaft.

- Don't add lead tape or drill holes in clubheads to "customize" the feel of the weighting. Doing this will distort the design properties and performance possibilities. Manufacturers spend tremendous sums of money on research and development; thus, top-grade clubs shouldn't be altered.

- Don't succumb to the temptation to order equipment advertised on infomercials. Put trust in your PGA Professional or coach to advise you on equipment.

ADDITIONAL EQUIPMENT NEEDS

Shoes play a considerable role in your performance. Make certain that your shoes are comfortable, provide excellent support and have good traction. Have at least two pairs of shoes, alternate each day, and use shoe trees so that they maintain their shape longer. Also change the spikes at least twice per season. High-quality rain gear is also essential. Get a breathable rain suit that will keep you dry and is comfortable to swing in. And don't forget to pack rain gloves in your bag. Distance-measuring devices that conform to USGA standards are often legal in competition and are excellent for everyday

EQUIPMENT AND GOLF BALLS, WHAT'S IN THE BAG?

List all of your equipment, including golf balls and other ancillary items, you're currently using.
Please note on the chart if your equipment has been professionally fitted and if it's suitable to you.

EQUIPMENT	DESCRIPTION	SUITABILITY
DRIVER		☐ Yes ☐ No
Shaft		☐ Yes ☐ No
FAIRWAY METALS		☐ Yes ☐ No
Shafts		☐ Yes ☐ No
IRONS		☐ Yes ☐ No
Shafts		☐ Yes ☐ No
WEDGES		☐ Yes ☐ No
Lofts		☐ Yes ☐ No
PUTTER		☐ Yes ☐ No
Length		☐ Yes ☐ No
BALLS		☐ Yes ☐ No
SHOES		☐ Yes ☐ No
GLOVES		☐ Yes ☐ No
Size		☐ Yes ☐ No
BAG		☐ Yes ☐ No
MISC.		☐ Yes ☐ No

play and practice rounds; all competitive golfers should have one. A SkyCaddie GPS unit is a worthwhile investment for the competitive golfer, as it's great to use in practice rounds and is legal in play when approved by the Tournament Committee.

10

THE RULES OF GOLF AND AMATEUR STATUS

*"Study the rules so that you won't beat yourself
by not knowing something."*

—Babe Didrikson Zaharias, World Golf Hall of Fame

In August 2008, Oklahoma State golfer Trent Leon learned a painful lesson about the Rules of Golf. An honorable mention All-America selection the previous season, Trent had just shot 2-under par to take a three-shot lead after the second round of the Canadian Men's Amateur Championship. As he entered the scoring tent area, he was distracted by a newspaper reporter who asked to interview him. Trent obliged by jumping over the boundary rope of the scoring area before he signed his scorecard. He was immediately disqualified because he broke a rule (Rule 6-6b, Signing and Returning Score Card) stating that a player must sign his card before leaving the scoring area. Just a few weeks earlier, Michelle Wie had also been disqualified for doing the exact same thing after the second round of the LPGA's State Farm Classic.

Not knowing the Rules of Golf can cost you strokes, and it can get you disqualified, as Leon and Wie discovered. It's

---

RULES CUSTODIANS

The USGA, Royal and Ancient Golf Club of St. Andrews (R&A), and the Royal Canadian Golf Association (RCGA) are the worldwide custodians of the Rules of Golf. Every serious golfer should have a USGA Rules Book and USGA Decisions Book, which they can find at usga.org. A full version of the Rules of Golf is available on the website, as well as video showing how the rules and decisions are applied. Players should always double-check to see that they're using the most recent version of the official Rules and Decisions books. The Rules of Golf is published every four years and the Decisions Book every other year.

---

your job to have a clear understanding of the Rules and how to apply them correctly. The Rules of Golf are designed to protect the integrity of a competition and its players. Golf is unique in the sporting world in that golfers are responsible for knowing the Rules and policing themselves. Understanding the Rules and how to apply them will give you the confidence of knowing that you'll likely avoid unnecessary penalties or disqualification.

The Rules can seem confusing, but they're designed to help you play the game fairly. They're easy to understand if you take a little bit of time to learn them. Get a Rules book from the United States Golf Association (USGA) and familiarize yourself with some of the "need to know" Rules highlighted in this chapter.

RULES YOU NEED TO KNOW

It's frustrating enough when things aren't going your way on the course. Everyone has days when their timing is off, their swing isn't in sync or their putts aren't falling in. That's golf. But don't let any rules infraction make the game even more painful. Nothing is more frustrating than having to post a score higher than you deserve, or being disqualified because of an error regarding the rules, procedure or protocol. Most rules infractions are avoidable, so take time to learn the rules. Having a sound working knowledge of the Rules will give you the confidence to play without fear of being penalized for a situation that could've been averted or dealt with more effectively. It can also work to your advantage when taking relief from ground under repair, obstructions and other conditions that allow you to improve your lie. Here are a few of the basic Rules that everyone should know.

Count your Clubs

In golf, you may play with 14 clubs in your bag, but no more. So the first thing you should do on the first tee is count your clubs. If an extra club sneaks into your bag on the practice green or range, and you don't discover it before you tee off, you'll be penalized. This very mistake cost Ian Woosnam a chance to win the 2001 British Open. Woosnam was leading the championship when he discovered he had 15 clubs in his bag on the second hole of the final round. Woosnam neglected to take his backup driver out of his bag after he finished warming up, and was penalized two strokes. Woosnam eventually wound up finishing third. The penalty in stroke play is two strokes for each hole played with the extra club(s), with a maximum penalty of four strokes lost per round. In match play, the penalty is a deduction of one hole for each hole played in breach of the rule, with a maximum deduction of two holes per round.

Read the Local Rules Sheet

Local rules sheets are critical for the event in which you're competing. It contains rules that apply to the competition and the course being played. Don't assume the local rules are the same everywhere you play and just throw them in your bag. Consider: On the final hole of the 2010 PGA Championship, Dustin Johnson was penalized two shots for grounding his club in what was deemed to be a bunker. Spectators were standing in the bunker just moments earlier, which might've thrown Johnson off, but item No. 1 on the local rules sheet given to players that week clearly stated that all bunkers on the course were designated as sand bunkers. Johnson, who led by one shot at the time, wound up making bogey (a triple bogey after the penalty) and missing a playoff by two shots.

Ask a Rules Official

Had Johnson asked an on-course rules official about the condition of the bunker, he might've gone on to win the championship. Most competitions have on-course rules officials; therefore, if you're unsure about how to proceed, call for a rules official. When you do seek advice, there are two questions you need to ask before you do anything:

1. *Are you a rules official?*
   This may sound silly, but there are plenty of course marshals and volunteers who are willing to help out. If they're not a rules official, do not take their advice.
2. *What are my options?*
   Under the Rules of Golf, you may be eligible to proceed in several different ways. Some rules officials will provide you only with answers to your specific

questions. By keeping your inquiry open-ended, the rules official will be able to provide you with all your options. Who knows, you may get a break you didn't know you were entitled to. If you're still not convinced that you're getting a correct ruling, ask for a second opinion. A good rules official will not be offended if you ask for additional help. In this instance, the ruling from the second official will be the one that stands.

In stroke play competition, you have another option if no rules official is available and you're unsure of how to proceed. Rule 3-3 allows you to play a second ball, providing you follow the correct procedure:

1. You announce to your fellow competitor or marker that you're going to play a second ball.
2. You announce which ball you would like to count, if the Rules permit.
3. You report the facts to the Committee before signing your scorecard.

Speak Up Immediately About Rules Violations

It is the duty of all competitors to make sure that everyone plays within the rules. This may be uncomfortable and awkward, but to protect the integrity of the competition you must confront any issues that arise in your group.

In match play, if you're concerned your opponent may have breached the Rules, you must advise your opponent immediately and tell him or her that you want the Rules of Golf to apply. Claims must be made in a timely fashion. Late claims will not be considered by the Rules Committee unless

QUIZ YOURSELF
Looking for a rules quiz? Check out the Royal Canadian Golf Association's website at rulesofgolf.ca. When you can successfully complete Level II of the quiz, you will have sufficient knowledge of the rules you need as a competitor.

they're made based on facts previously unknown to you, and you've been given wrong information by your opponent. (See Rule 2-5: Doubt as to Procedure; Disputes and Claims)

You're Responsible for Your Caddie

Any breach of the Rules by your caddie results in a penalty to you. Also, when searching for a ball that may be lost, don't let your caddie begin the search before you get there. The five minutes allowed for searching starts as soon as you or your caddie begins searching.

Take Care of Your Scorecard

Golfers are responsible for handing in their official scorecard immediately after the completion of play, signed and attested to by their fellow competitors. Don't be in a rush. Take your time and double check your scorecard before you hand it in. Make sure that the correct score is recorded clearly in the box for each hole that you played. You're not responsible for adding the scores.

THE RULES OF AMATEUR STATUS

It's crucial to understand the Rules of Amateur Status so that you don't jeopardize your ability to play in amateur competitions. You must be an amateur to be eligible to play collegiate golf and receive scholarships. Consult the USGA, R&A or RCGA if you have any questions about amateur status. Rules for amateur status are found in a special section of the USGA Rules of Golf on Amateur Status. The following information is courtesy of the USGA:

An amateur golfer must not take any action for the purpose of becoming a professional golfer and must not identify himself as a professional golfer. Such actions include applying for a professional's position; directly or indirectly receiving services or payment from a professional agent or sponsor, commercial or otherwise; directly or indirectly entering into a written or oral agreement with a professional agent or sponsor, commercial or otherwise; and agreeing to accept payment or compensation for allowing one's name or likeness as a player of golf skill or reputation to be used for any commercial purpose.

There are two exceptions to the USGA's restrictions: 1) If you apply unsuccessfully for an assistant professional position, and 2) if you enter and play in any stage of a competition to qualify for a professional tour, provided you waive your right to any prize money.

Once you're familiar with the entire section, there are a few rules you should particularly note in the section on Amateur Status:

RULE 6: Use of Golf Skill or Reputation
Except as provided in the Rules, an amateur golfer can't use his or her skills or reputation to promote, advertise or sell anything or for any financial gain.

RULE 6-2: Lending Name or Likeness
An amateur can't use his or her skills or reputation

to obtain payment, compensation, personal benefit or any financial gain for allowing his name or likeness to be used for the advertisement or sale of anything. An amateur golfer can accept equipment from equipment manufacturers or dealers provided no advertising is involved.

RULE 6-3: Personal Appearance

An amateur can't use his or her skills or reputation to obtain payment, compensation, personal benefit or any financial gain for a personal appearance, except for reasonable expenses if no golf competition or exhibition is involved.

RULE 6-4: Broadcasting and Writing

An amateur can't use his or her skills or reputation to obtain payment, compensation, personal benefit or any financial gain for broadcasting or writing about golf unless it's their primary occupation, they're writing or broadcasting on a part-time basis, or they're the actual author of the book, article or commentary. In no instance can the writing or broadcasting discuss instruction on how to play the game.

RULE 6-5: Grants and Scholarships

An amateur can't use his or her skills or reputation to gain the benefits of a scholarship or grant-in-aid other than in accord with the regulations of the NCAA, the Association of Intercollegiate Athletics for Women, the NAIA, the NJCAA or other similar organizations governing athletes at academic institutions.

RULE 6-6: Membership

An amateur can't accept membership or privileges in a club or at a course without full payment for the membership when the membership or privileges are offered because of the player's golf skill or reputation. Membership or privileges can be accepted when they've been awarded as purely and deservedly honorary, in recognition of an outstanding performance, without any time limit and at no charge to anyone.

RULE 4: Managing Your Expenses

Rule 4 in the Amateur Status section is a lengthy rule that you'd best read in full, but in general states that it's acceptable to receive reasonable expenses to play in competition from several sources, including your family or legal guardian, or from a golf club or association to play in a team competition. You should contact the USGA or your state golf association if you have questions about accepting expense money or other forms of financial support. Here are a few rules regarding expenses that could affect you:

RULE 4-2C/D: Golf Club and Golf Association Team Competitions

An amateur representing a golf club or golf association in a team practice session (within limits fixed by the USGA) and/or team competition between golf clubs or golf associations can accept expenses through the golf clubs or golf associations involved. A member of a visiting team in such a team competition can accept expenses to the national amateur championship of the host association when the championship immediately precedes or follows the team competition.

RULE 4-2E: Invitation Unrelated to Golf Skill

An amateur who is invited for reasons unrelated to golf skill (as a celebrity, a business associate or customer, a guest in a club-sponsored competition, winner of a random drawing, etc.) to take part in a golf event can accept expenses.

RULE 5: Instruction

Except as provided in the Rules, an amateur can't receive payment or compensation for giving golf instruction. There are few exceptions, including the following:

RULE 5-2: Where Payment Permitted

Payment is permitted if you're an employee of an educational institution (i.e., a high school gym teacher) receiving compensation for instruction to students. You can also receive payment as a camp counselor. An amateur can receive expenses, not exceeding the actual expenses incurred, for giving golf instruction to junior golfers as part of a program that has been approved by the USGA.

RULE 3: Prizes

An amateur must not play golf for prize money or its equivalent in a match, tournament or exhibition. A player can participate in an event in which prize money or its equivalent is offered, provided that prior to participation he waives his right to accept prize money. There are some exceptions and limitations.

RULE 3-2: Prize Money

The rules state that an amateur must not accept a prize (including all prizes received in any one tournament or exhibition for any event, or series of events, in which golf skill is a factor) of a retail value greater than 500 sterling (R&A), $750 (USGA) or $1,000 (RCGA), except for symbolic prizes. A "symbolic prize" is a trophy made of gold, silver, ceramic, glass or the like that is permanently and distinctively engraved. A prize, including a cash prize, for a hole-in-one made while playing golf may exceed the above prize limit. An amateur also cannot accept a prize of money or the equivalent of money over the above amounts, or convert a prize (say, a gift certificate) into cash. An amateur also cannot accept expenses in any amount to a golf competition (except as provided in Rule 4), or money to appear or play in an event because of golf skill or reputation. Essentially, an amateur golfer cannot accept any prizes that might exceed a value of $750 (under USGA Rules), except in the case of a hole-in-one or a symbolic prize. Also, an amateur golfer may not accept payments in the form of compensation or expenses for golfing activities.

RULE 3-3: Testimonial Awards

An amateur golfer must not accept a testimonial award of a retail value greater than $750 (USGA). What is a testimonial award? It's an award for notable performances or contributions to golf as distinguished from competition prizes. A testimonial award may not be a monetary award. However, an amateur can accept more than one testimonial award from different

LOSS OF STATUS, GAMBLING AND MORE

The rules for Amateur Status also include rules on how to dress, professionalism and what to do if you have lost your status and wish to regain it. There's also more information on playing for prize money. See the USGA Policy on Gambling in the rules book or at usga.org for further explanation.

donors, even if their total retail value exceeds $750 (USGA), provided they're not presented so as to evade the limit for a single award.

TAP INS

Five-time British Open champion Tom Watson said,

"One way to learn the Rules of Golf is to hit the books. Another way is to play the game and suffer the penalties called on yourself. There is no surer nor [more] painful way to learn a rule than to be penalized for breaking it."

Avoid that kind of pain: Become knowledgeable about the Rules and confident in applying them when you play.

Conclusion

High Performance Golf provides serious athletes interested in exploring their limits as competitive golfers with a framework to accompany them on their journey. Take full advantage of the information presented. See yourself as a winner. Put in the necessary effort in the appropriate areas. Navigate through the inevitable rough patches. And, finally, surround yourself with an outstanding support team who believes in you and wants you to succeed. You'll never lose. Good luck!

"Success is peace of mind which is a direct result of self-satisfaction in knowing you made the effort to become the best you are capable of becoming."

Coach John Wooden
ESPN "Coach of the Century"
Coach of 10 NCAA Championship Teams

About Henry Brunton

Henry Brunton is one of the most recognizable names in Canadian golf and is one of the world's leading golf coaches and educators. He was the Royal Canadian Golf Association's National Golf Coach from 1999-2011, the creator of the PGA of Canada's Teaching and Coaching Certification Program, a PGA of Canada Master Professional and the only Canadian listed among *GOLF Magazine*'s Top 100 Teachers in America. In 2009, he published *Journey to Excellence: The Young Goalfer's Complete Guide to Achievement and Personal Growth*, the first comprehensive guide to competitive junior golf for both juniors and their parents.

A graduate of the University of Ottawa, Brunton has been a member of the PGA of Canada since 1984. In 2008, the PGA of Canada honored him with its highest standing —Master Professional. He was also named as the fourth Most Influential Person in Canadian Golf in rankings by Canada's *National Post*.

Brunton has a passion for developing elite junior golfers. He was Canada's National Coach since the Royal Canadian Golf Association established its Player Development Program in 1999, and held the position until 2011. Teams led by Brunton won the 2001 Four Nations Cup Championship and the 2003 Americas Cup and have competed for Canada around the globe. Brunton coached the Canadian National

Men's Team to a Silver Medal finish at the 2006 World Amateur Championship in South Africa, and the Canadian Junior Team to a Bronze Medal finish in the 2010 World Junior Championship in Japan.

In 1999 he was hired by the PGA of Canada to design and develop a national teacher and coach education program. The result was the highly acclaimed Teaching and Coaching Certification Program (TCCP). The TCCP is a mandatory training program for all PGA of Canada Professionals.

Brunton is an accomplished speaker and consultant. He has been a featured presenter at golf conferences throughout Canada as well as in Australia, Germany, England, Bermuda, Puerto Rico, Japan, Trinidad and Tobago, in the United States for various PGA Sections, at the prestigious "Better Golf Through Technology" Conference at MIT in Cambridge, Massachusetts. In 2009 he was a keynote speaker at the PGA Teaching and Coaching Summit in Port. St. Lucie, Florida. In 2010 Brunton was a featured speaker at the World Golf Fitness Summit in Orlando, Florida as well as the British PGA Junior Golf Summit at the Belfry. In 2011 he delivered keynote addresses at the PGA of America Inaugural Junior Golf Summit at Pinehurst and at the English Golfing Union Coaches Summit in Birmingham, UK. In 2012, he presented his research paper at the World Scientific Congress of Golf VI in Phoenix, Arizona. He is also an Advisory Board Member of the Titleist Performance Institute (TPI), the Journal of Applied Golf Research (JAGR) and The First Tee.

In 2005, Brunton was the first and only Canadian recognized by GOLF Magazine as one of America's "Top 100 Teachers," the publication's survey of teaching excellence. In 2008 he became the first Canadian to be included among the U.S. Kids Golf Top 50 Junior Teachers list. In 2009 he was named

National Junior Leader of the Year by the PGA of Canada. In 2010 Brunton was the first Canadian recognized by the PGAs of Europe—an alliance of PGAs of 37 countries—with its most prestigious honor, the Five Star Professional Award. In 2012 Brunton was named U.S. Kids Golf Master Junior Teacher, the first Canadian to be so recognized.

Henry Brunton Golf is based at Eagles Nest Golf Club near Toronto, Canada. Winter programs are conducted at the Metro Golf Dome in Toronto and at the PGA Center for Learning and Performance in Port St. Lucie, Florida.

www.henrybrunton.com